A Young Man in Search of Love

By Isaac Bashevis Singer

THE FAMILY MOSKAT

SATAN IN GORAY

GIMPEL THE FOOL

THE SPINOZA OF MARKET STREET

THE MAGICIAN OF LUBLIN

THE SLAVE

SHORT FRIDAY AND OTHER STORIES

THE MANOR

THE ESTATE

THE SEANCE

A FRIEND OF KAFKA

A CROWN OF FEATHERS

IN MY FATHER'S COURT

ENEMIES, A LOVE STORY

PASSIONS

A Young Man in Search of Love

Isaac Bashevis Singer
Paintings and Drawings by
RAPHAEL SOYER

1978
Doubleday & Company, Inc., Garden City, New York

Library of Congress Cataloging in Publication Data

Singer, Isaac Bashevis, 1904–
    A young man in search of love.

    1. Singer, Isaac Bashevis, 1904–   —Biography
—Youth. 2. Author, Yiddish—Biography.   I.   Ti-
tle.
PJ5129.S49Z528   839'.09'33   [B]
ISBN: 0-385-12357-4
Library of Congress Catalog Card Number 77–2538

In a way, this book is a continuation of *A Little Boy in Search of God,* but it is also a story in itself—a story of the never-ceasing search and gain of love. Together, these two volumes constitute a kind of spiritual autobiography which I hope to continue in the years to come.

For me, religion and love, even sex, are attributes of the same substance, as they were for the Kabbalists of all generations. The Godhead itself is a union of the principles of male and female, a yearning which can never be completely fulfilled.

I am lucky to have as the illustrator of this book my great friend the artist Raphael Soyer. My thanks to him, and to my young editor, Eve Roshevsky, as well as to my nephew Joseph Singer, who did the translation of this work.

I.B.S.

LIST OF ILLUSTRATIONS

Drawings

Frontispiece

Color Plates

(Following page 68)

(Following page 100)

A Young Man in Search of Love

1

I.

I had more or less settled again in Warsaw, the city of my dreams and hopes. I was a proofreader for a literary magazine, which gave me an opportunity to be in contact with writers and intellectuals. I even acquired a mistress, Gina, perhaps twice as old as I but a woman whom I could love and from whom I could learn. In a moment of exaltation I had promised her that we would have a child together, but the forces that rule the world didn't want Gina to be the mother of my child. We lived together, but she didn't conceive. I quickly realized that she was even older than I thought. Among her things I found photographs showing her dressed in fashions prevailing before I was even born. She still had her periods, but not regularly. Yes, this woman might easily have been my mother, but not the mother of my child.

My literary and my other troubles were such that I no longer fretted about my romantic complications. I had presented myself for conscription and had been given a "B" classification which under the Russians had been called a green ticket. This meant that I had to present myself again a year hence. During the few hours I spent with the conscripts I got a taste of the army. Some soldiers ordered us around as if we were already part of it. The Christians already cursed the Jewish conscripts and called them all kinds of names. The Jewish youths tried to curry favor with the gentiles, paid them compliments, offered them cigarettes and chocolate, and even pressed coins upon them. Stripping naked in front of a crowd was to me a travail. My skin was unusually white, and my hair as red as fire. Someone gave me a slap in the rear, another flicked my nose, a third called me: "slob, jerk."

The soldier who was temporarily my superior measured me head to toe and from toe to head, made comical gestures, and remarked: "Woe to the Polish nation if this has to be her defender."

This evoked a burst of wild laughter. The notion that I might be spending two years among this crew drove me into despair. I looked on with amazement as the other youths somehow made peace with their situation and did their best to adjust. They quickly assumed a military tone; they even made fun of me on their own initiative. A tall youth with a heroic physique came up to me and said: "Are you a mama's boy? The army will make a man of you. Have a cigarette."

I grew so befuddled that I stuck the wrong end of the cigarette in my mouth, which brought a new howl of laughter and applause. The boys had already tagged me with a nickname: *Ofermo,* which was applied to an inept soldier. I sidled over into a corner and mentally vented all my complaints, not against the people who insulted me but against God. What resentments could one hold against these youths? They had been raised in the streets, and nature had endowed them with the ability to adapt to difficult situations instead of breaking. But the creator of the universe should have had more decency than to subject young men of my nature to such degradations. I had made a firm resolution that if I were taken, I would commit suicide despite the fact that this would forever darken my mother's years, she whose bashfulness, pride, and rebelliousness against the laws of life I had inherited. I also toyed with the notion of killing her first before putting an end to myself.

The two military doctors who examined me didn't concur. One was of the frank opinion that I had intentionally starved myself which had brought about my weakened condition. The other waved his hand as if to say: "Let him wander around a bit longer." After I had dressed and the other conscripts learned that I had been deferred for a year, they seemed astounded. In their estimation I should have been classified "D," which meant rejection even during a time of war. One of the wise guys who had already begun to fraternize with the soldiers and speak their jargon had been freed with the classification I should have gotten.

When I came out into the street and glanced into a mirror in the front window of a furniture store, I was frightened at my own appearance. I looked emaciated as if from

consumption, pale, and like someone who has just narrowly escaped death. I felt light, hollow, and it seemed to me that my feet were racing downhill as if of their own accord. Now that I was temporarily freed from the fear of military service, I began to agonize about my literary efforts. I had already been writing for several years but sooner or later I had thrown my manuscripts into the wastebasket. The themes employed by Yiddish writers and the writing itself struck me as sentimental, primitive, petty. Too often it had to do with a girl whose parents wanted an arranged marriage while she really loved someone else. Quite often the girl came from a wealthy family and the youth was the son of a tailor or shoemaker. Would it be possible to describe in Yiddish the kind of relationship I had with Gina? Although Yiddish literature flirted with socialism and more recently with communism, it had remained provincial and backward. Besides, Yiddish—the language itself—had become repugnant both to gentiles and to a great number of modern Jews. Even such Yiddish writers as Mendele Moher Sforim, Sholem Aleichem, and Peretz called Yiddish a jargon. The Zionists considered Yiddish the language of the Diaspora of which the Jews had to divest themselves along with the exile. I knew enough Hebrew to attempt writing in that language but at that time few people spoke Hebrew. It lacked words used in day-to-day conversation. Ben Yehuda was just on the verge of creating the new Hebrew. Writing in Hebrew

R·S·

meant constantly consulting dictionaries and trying to recall sentences from the Scriptures, the Mishnah, and the
Gemara. Both the Yiddish literature and the Hebrew
avoided the great adventures inherent in Jewish history—
the false Messiahs, the expulsions, the forcible conversions,
the Emancipation, and the assimilations that had created a
condition in which Jews became ministers in England,
Italy, and America; professors in large universities; million-
aires; party leaders; editors of world-famous newspapers.
Yiddish literature ignored the Jewish underworld, the
thousands and tens of thousands of thieves, pimps, pros-
titutes, and white slavers in Buenos Aires, Rio de Ja-
neiro, and even in Warsaw. Yiddish literature reminded me
of my father's courtroom where almost everything was forbidden. True, Sholem Asch had in a sense created a minor
revolution and had taken up themes that till then had been
considered taboo, but he was and remained a rustic, at least
that's how I saw him then and still do to this day. His stories personified the pathos of the provincial who has been
shown the big world for the first time and who describes it
when he goes back to the town where he came from.

The problem was that in order to write with skill about
people of the world, one needed to know the world, and I
only knew a small segment of Jewish Warsaw, Bilgoray,
and two or three other small towns. I only knew Jews that
spoke Yiddish. Even then I knew a writer can only write
about people and things he knows well.

I had promised to let Gina and my brother Joshua know what had happened to me but neither he nor she had a telephone at that time. I went to the Writers Club and everything there was just as usual. Several journalists played chess. Others read newspapers that came there from all over Poland and from abroad. I knew everyone here and each of his idiosyncrasies. One of them, an old writer named Saks who came from Lodz and who had lived for a time in Central Asia, waged a private feud against the Allies for having wronged Germany. He hurled fire and brimstone upon the Versailles Treaty for taking Upper Silesia away from the Germans and creating the corridor between East and West Germany. In prophetic terms he predicted that Germany would one day rearm and take everything back. By this time Hitler had already conducted his famous *Putsch* and perhaps also published his *Mein Kampf*, but this Lodz Jew knew nothing of this, or maybe he ignored it. I would occasionally ask him:

"What did Germany ever do for you that you take up for her so? After all, we're Polish citizens, not German."

He would glance at me with bewilderment and reply:

"You can't take a great nation, a pillar of civilization, and dismember it."

If I'm not mistaken, this same journalist later died in a Nazi concentration camp.

I recalled Spinoza's words to the effect that everything could become a passion. I had resolved beforehand to be-

come a narrator of human passion rather than of a placid life-style.

Nearly everyone here at the Writers Club bore some passion and was blinded by it. The young writers all aspired to become literary geniuses and many of them were convinced that they already were except that the others refused to acknowledge their genius. The Communists waited impatiently for the social revolution to start so that they could exact revenge upon all the bourgeois, Zionists, Socialists, petit bourgeois, the lumpenproletariat, the clergy, and most of all, the editors who refused to publish them. The few women members were convinced that they were victims of male contempt for the female sex. One of the hangers-on here was an actor named Jaque Levi, who had made guest appearances with a troupe in Prague in 1911 and had become a close friend of Franz Kafka there. He often spoke of this Kafka of whom I had never heard. Jaque Levi walked around with pockets stuffed with yellowed letters from Kafka.

I would ask him: "Who is this Kafka?"

And he would point a finger and say:

"One day he will be world-famous!"

I did not want to discuss either the evils of the Versailles Treaty or Kafka's greatness, but Levi and Saks had to talk to someone. At that time, an actress used to come to the Writers Club with whom Kafka was allegedly in love—a Madam Tchizhik. She had performed with Jaque Levi in

Prague. It was hard to believe that anyone could be in love with this woman, but I told myself that the passions—like Leibnitz's monads—had no windows.

Gina never came to the Writers Club for I had forbidden her to do so. I was too shy to be seen with her by the older writers. I felt that everyone would be able to tell from my face that we were having an affair. Most of all I was ashamed before my elder brother with his knowledge of life and sense of irony. My shyness at that time assumed the character of a neurosis.

2.

Sitting that day at the Writers Club, I took yet another accounting of my life. I had barely missed being conscripted that day. I had seen this clearly in the doctors' eyes. A year hence, I would have to present myself again and I lacked the strength to subject myself to further weeks and months of deprivation. My brother suggested that the best solution for me would be to go to the Land of Israel. Maybe I could obtain a certificate from the Palestine Bureau in Warsaw which issued the few certificates that the English Mandate Authority allotted for Jewish immigrants. But what would I do in Palestine? Physical laborers were needed there, not a young man who was trying to write stories and in Yiddish besides. I had met several youths and girls who had gone to the Land of Israel and had come back disillusioned and sick with malaria. They

RAPHAEL
SOYER

told frightening stories about the privation, the unhealthy climate, the bureaucracy of the English as well as the Jewish officials, the exploitation by the contractors who did the hiring, and the dangers posed by the Arabs. In those days, Yiddish was an anthema in Palestine. Hebraist fanatics invaded meetings in institutions where Yiddish was spoken.

My own concerns were promptly transformed within me into consideration of the world condition. I no longer believed that God had issued the Torah on Mount Sinai along with all the innovations and restrictions that commentators and exegetes had added in every generation. Whether God was a substance with infinite attributes, or the absolute, or blind will, or whatever the philosophers chose to call Him, one couldn't depend on His justice and mercy. I could never forget the tens of millions of people who had perished in the World War, in the Bolshevik Revolution, in the pogroms, the famines, the epidemics. Millions of peasants in Russia had been labeled kulaks and exiled to Siberia. Whole villages had been starved out. There was fighting in China, in Manchuria. In generation after generation people sacrificed their lives in battle, but nothing was ever realized. How did one become a writer in such a universal slaughterhouse? How could I write about love while millions of innocent creatures writhed in the clutches of slaughterers, hunters, and vivisectionists of every ilk? I imagined that I heard the sound of all the living through all the ages. I had been freed for a year but countless other young men had to begin learning to kill and be killed while enduring the insults and blows of those a rank higher.

I knew full well that Gina was waiting for me but I somehow didn't feel like going home. I owed her months of back rent. I had begun to grow weary of her pathos, her endless assurances that she was in constant touch with the dead, her hunger for love that I could never manage to satisfy. However many compliments I paid her, she still demanded more. She suffered from a terrible inferiority complex (a term I had first heard a short time before). She constantly demanded my avowals of eternal love. She kept saying that she was ready to lay down her life for me—as well as with me—but I neither needed her to die for me nor was ready to enter into a suicide pact with her. During the months that I had been depleting myself I had given in to all her sexual desires. This had been a means of losing weight and strength. Now I was so sated with sex that I longed for a night when I could sleep alone. I was overcome by a fatigue and a feeling that my end was near.

With my last groschen I had ordered something to eat from the buffet at the Writers Club. I was joined at the table by several fledgling writers, each with his own plans, complaints, vexations. One had been left out by a critic who had compiled a list of prose writers of the younger generation in a literary journal. A second had been promised to have his poem printed by an editor but months had gone by

and the poem still lay in the editor's drawer, or possibly he had lost it. A third needed an operation and was getting ready to enter a hospital. A fourth told a joke about a man who went to a brothel, found himself impotent, and was scolded by the Madam for coming on a Sabbath when the house was so full of patrons.

I chewed my sausage, mused that a cow or steer had paid with its life for it, smiled at the joke, tried to console the writer whose prestige had been so neglected, and wished the sick colleague a speedy recovery knowing all the while that the writer lacked talent and the sick man had no chance of recovery. We all clutched at something that a knife, a drop of poison, or a rope could curtail in less than a minute. We were all cursed with that self-love that no blows or disappointments can diminish, and of which one is freed only with one's final breath.

On the way home, I stopped before the window of a bookstore. I was preparing to write books yet the world was inundated with books. Thick, dusty volumes lined the store from floor to ceiling. I had bought a Yiddish newspaper in which a writer waged a polemic against the Polish anti-Semites who accused the Jews of trying to dominate the world. The chief anti-Semite, Adam Novoczynski, had tried for the countless time to prove to his readers that the Elders of Zion, the Masons, Stalin, Trotsky, Leon Blum, the Rabbi of Gora, Weizman, Mussolini, and Hitler were part of one big conspiracy to dismember and again partition

the newly founded Polish nation. Novoczynski also included Pilsudski in this cabal, he who a few years earlier had won the war against the Bolsheviks. The Yiddish newspaper demanded logic. I had read this writer on more than one occasion. He had such an ability to arouse the emotions that reading him, I myself grew as if temporarily hypnotized by his style, his passion, his paranoid suspicions.

When I came home, Gina assailed me with recriminations. Where had I been all day? Why hadn't I let her know the good news? True she knew that I was free since her dead grandmother had revealed herself to her and informed her, but where had I been all these hours? My behavior had given Gina a headache and she had to take aspirin or some other pills. She had prepared lunch for me but it had grown cold. She kissed me and scolded me. She accused me of unfaithfulness and predicted that I would treat her the same way the other men before me had done. She was ready to forgive me everything and conduct a sexual orgy with me but the moment I lay down I fell into a sleep from which no caresses or quarrels could rouse me.

2

For a while it appeared that Yiddish and Yiddish literature were making progress. Great numbers of pious youths in the small towns had laid aside their Gemaras and begun reading Yiddish newspapers and books. A number of new publishers and magazines had cropped up. In every sizable city a Yiddish weekly or monthly now appeared. The literary magazine where I was proofreader had been taken over by a big publisher—the house of Kletzkin. The proprietor, Boris Kletzkin, a wealthy man and a patron of Yiddish literature, had rented quarters in Simon's Passage at 52 Nalewki Street which included a book warehouse, Yiddish typewriters, telephones, bookkeepers, a cashier, a director, and other employees. My salary was raised slightly and I could now give Gina something toward the rent as well as pay for my meals. As if this weren't enough, my brother Israel Joshua enjoyed a sudden windfall—he was appointed Polish correspondent for the American Yiddish newspaper *The Jewish Daily Forward*. In the period since the World War the Yiddishist movement in America had flourished. A whole literature had evolved there. The *Forward* was the largest Yiddish newspaper in America and had about a

quarter of a million readers, which for a Yiddish newspaper was an enormous circulation. The Yiddish Theater presented a number of better plays. The editor of the *Forward*, Abe Cahan, who also wrote in English and was considered something of a classicist in American literature, ruled the paper with an iron hand. The *Forward*, which was closely connected with the Workmen's Circle and with many trade unions, had its own ten-story building on East Broadway. One day, Abe Cahan happened to read my brother's collection of short stories entitled *Pearls* and was inspired by the writing. He promptly invited my brother to publish his literary works in the *Forward* and soon afterward, he appointed him its Polish correspondent. My brother's salary came to about fifty dollars a week, but in those days fifty dollars was a considerable sum when exchanged into Polish zlotys. Literary and journalist Warsaw seethed over my brother's success.

In the first years following the Revolution, the *Forward*, a socialist newspaper, had expressed sympathy toward communism. But Abe Cahan quickly realized that he had erred and the *Forward* became sharply anti-Communist, actually the most important anti-Bolshevik newspaper in America. The *Forward* writers, most of whom were experts on all the radical movements in Russia, uncovered Stalin's murders long before the democratic world became aware of them. The *Forward* would arrive at the Writers Club and I read it. America was enjoying "prosperity" (one of the English words that American-Yiddish adopted). Jews grew wealthy from real estate, from stocks that kept ever climbing, and from various other businesses. The *Forward* printed stories and novels by the best Yiddish writers as well as articles written by prominent non-Jewish socialists and liberals in Europe. The people at the Writers Club laughed at the somewhat anglicized Yiddish employed in the *Forward,* yet they all strove to work for this affluent newspaper which paid generous fees.

A second child had been born to my brother—Joseph, or Yosele (who is now the translator of most of my works). My brother had rented a comfortable apartment at 36 Leszno Street. One day he was a pauper; the next, he was considered rich by the indigent literary community. He wanted to help me, but I had resolved to live on my earnings. I actually avoided him, and the reason for this was my shyness. Known writers and young women who were admirers of literature used to congregate at his home. Most of these young women came from wealthy homes, were fashionably dressed, smoked cigarettes, spoke a good Polish, laughed loudly, and kissed the men, and I was ashamed before them with my cheap clothes, my broken Polish, and my Yeshiva-student-like bashfulness. They were all older than I and they discussed me as if I were some curiosity. They would point their manicured fingers and ask: "Wherever did he get such fiery red hair? Do you notice how blue his eyes are?"

It was enough for a woman to merely glance at me to make me blush deeply. At Gina's house I was a mighty lover, but here I again became a child, a heder boy. This double role confused me and evoked astonishment among others, since it was known that I wrote and had a mistress. In some book or magazine, I had stumbled upon a phrase: "split personality," and I applied this diagnosis to myself. This was precisely what I was—cloven, torn, perhaps a single body with many souls each pulling in a different direction. I lived like a libertine yet I didn't cease praying to God and asking for His mercy; I broke every law of the Shulhan Arukh and at the same time I read cabala books and Hasidic volumes; I had spotted the weaknesses in the famous philosophers and great writers yet I wrote things that emerged naïve, awkward, amateurish. Now my potency was beyond belief—suddenly I became impotent. Some kind of enemy roosted within me or a dybbuk who spited me in every way and played cat-and-mouse with me. As soon as I read of some phobia or neurosis, I immediately acquired it. All the afflictions psychiatrists and neurologists described in their works assailed me one after another and often, all at the same time. I was consumptive, had cancer in my intestines, a tumor in my brain, I was growing blind, deaf, paralyzed, insane. I suffered from nightmares and compulsions. Some maniac uttered crazy words inside my brain and I could not silence him. At the same time I held myself in such check that not even Gina knew what I was

going through. Older writers at the Writers Club often told me they envied my youth and I said: "Believe me, there is nothing to envy."

I sought in books a solution to my distraction (and to all other enigmas). I constantly browsed through bookstores and libraries, but the books nearly all disappointed me, even the works of masters. The philosophers all made claims whose truths they couldn't substantiate. What's more, even if what they said were true, I found no new data there and certainly no solace. The literary works, the novels, all concurred that a man could love just one woman at a time and vice versa. But I felt that they lied. Rather than literature denying men's laws, the laws had seized literature in a trap and kept it there. I frequently fantasized about writing a novel in which the hero was simultaneously in love with a number of women. Since the Orientals were allowed to practice polygamy and to maintain harems (if they could afford it), the European could do the same. Monogamy was a law established by legislators, not by nature. But an artist had to be true to nature, human nature, at least in his descriptions regardless how wild, unjust, and insane it might be. Somewhere I had the suspicion that what was going on in my head went on in many other heads as well. Not only Yiddish literature but many other literatures struck me as too inhibited. Already then I had the feeling that every kind of censorship did great harm to literature. When I read *Anna Karenina,* I thought how good it would have been if Tolstoy could have described Anna's sexual relationships with her husband, and later, with her lover. All the details about Anna's dress, her visits, her friendships, and her journeys did little to reveal her situation. How much better it would have been to learn of her erotic relations with the two men; the crises and inhibitions that emerge in bed, when the person doffs not only his or her physical clothes but some of his spiritual ones as well. The sexual organs expressed more of the human soul than all the other body parts, even the eyes. To write about love and exclude sex was a useless labor.

Rummaging through the bookstores and libraries, I encountered a number of books that steered me in the direction I was to follow later. I found Professor Kraushaar's works about the False Messiah, Jacob Frank, and his disciples. I read whatever I could about the era of Sabbatai Zevi, in whose footsteps Jacob Frank had followed. I ran across many books that described the punishments imposed upon witches in Europe and America, the Crusades and their mass hysterias, as well as various accounts of dybbuks both Jewish and gentile. In these works I found everything I had been pondering—hysteria, sex, fanaticism, superstition. The fact was that in our house these subjects had always been discussed and analyzed.

My father thought the world of Rabbi Jonathan Eibeshutz and bore a grudge against Rabbi Jonathan's enemy, Reb Jacob Emden. Rabbi Jonathan's book *Tablet of the*

Testimony almost always lay on the desk of my father's study. Father often discussed with Mother (who was a scholarly woman) the fact that Rabbi Jonathan had been a just and pious man and that the accusations made against him by Reb Jacob Emden alleging that he, Rabbi Jonathan, was a secret follower of Sabbatai Zevi and that he issued amulets with allusions to Sabbatai Zevi and that he had brought down an epidemic and other misfortunes upon pregnant women, were false. Father constantly brought up Reb Jacob Emden's "Torat ha-Kenaot," "Edut beyaakob," "Shebirat Luhot ha-Aren," and his other tracts. Disputes between rabbis going back some two hundred years had more substance in our house than current events in the daily newspaper. Father believed every word written by the cabalists and waged a private war against those who openly or covertly contended that the Zohar hadn't been written by Rabbi Simon Ben Yohay but by Reb Moshe de Leon. One of the most outspoken opponents of the cabala had been the Italian scholar and exegete Reb Aryeh de Medina, and his name was anathema in our house.

Because my brother Joshua had become enlightened and Father was terrified lest the younger children follow his example, he constantly plied us with tales of transmigrated spirits, dybbuks, and miracles performed by various wonder-rabbis and saints. Somewhere inside Father nursed a resentment against Mother, who was inclined toward

logic and science and had even been slightly infected by
the Enlightenment. Her father, the Bilgoray rabbi, my
grandfather Reb Jacob Mordecai, thought highly of Jacob
Emden and was a bit of a *misnagid,* or anti-Hasid, and Father occasionally erupted with angry words against his
father-in-law. From childhood I had been steeped in Has-
idism, cabala, miracles, and all kinds of occult beliefs and
fantasies. After lengthy stumbling and groping I redis-
covered what I had been carrying within me the whole
time.

2.

Somewhere, I had heard or read the expression "the
reappraisal of all values" and it was clear to me that this
was what I had to do—reappraise all values. I could not
rely on any authority. I still hadn't published a single word
and at the Writers Club I was known only as "Singer's
brother." Just the same I waged contentions with God, the
Prophets, religions, philosophies, as well as with the crea-
tors of world literature. Was Shakespeare really the genius
he was made out to be? Were Maxim Gorki and Andreyev
pillars of literature? Were Mendele Moher Sforim, Peretz,
Sholem Aleichem, and Bialik really as great as the Yid-
dishists and Hebraists wanted them to be? Had Hegel
really said anything new in philosophy? Had the species
really originated as Darwin claimed they had? Was there

any substance to the assertions of Karl Marx, Lenin, Bukharin? Was democracy indeed the best system? Could a Jewish State in Palestine really solve the Jewish question? Did the words "equality" and "freedom" really mean something or were they mere rhetoric? Was it worthwhile to go on living and struggling in this world or were those who spat upon the whole mess right?

I was surrounded on all sides by the faithful who all believed in something: the Orthodox and the Zionists, the Hasidim and the *misnagdim*, the writers of the editorials in the Yiddish press and the anti-Semites in the Polish press, those who defended the League of Nations and those who opposed it. The brides and grooms who were congratulated in the newspapers apparently believed in the institution of marriage and in bringing forth new generations. I had often heard educators discussing the problems of rearing the young. In his letters to me, my father constantly warned me to live like a Jew and not—God forbid—forget or disgrace my heritage. Mother, on the other hand, pleaded again and again that I guard my health, not catch cold, God forbid, eat on time, go to sleep early, and not overwork. She wished me long life and hoped that I would make a good match and provide her with grandchildren. My sister-in-law Genia, Joshua's wife, often consulted with her sister, Bella, and with neighbors about which would be best for Yosele—to breast-feed him or give him a bottle, to use this formula or that? But something within me asked:

"What for? Why? Why slaughter chickens, calves, and kids and bring up people? Why slave and stay up nights so that there would be a Yosele, an Isaac, or a Gina?"

As skillful as Tolstoy was in portraying individual types, so naïve did he seem to me when he tried to give advice on how to solve the agrarian problem in Russia or to expedite the teaching of the Gospel. All this babble about a better to-morrow, a rosier future, a united mankind, or equality was based on wishes, delusions, and sometimes merely on lust for power. It was clear to me that after the First World War there would have to come a second, a third, a tenth. Most faces expressed callousness, supreme egotism, indifference to everything outside their own ken, and, quite often, stupidity. Here they prayed and there they slaughtered. The same priests who preached love on Sunday morning hunted a fox, a hare, or some other helpless creature on Sunday afternoon or tried to hook a fish in the Vistula. The Polish officers who strutted about displaying their medals, brandishing their swords, and saluting each other hadn't the slightest chance of defending their country if it were attacked by Russia or Germany. And it was just as hard to believe that England would surrender her mandate in Palestine or that the Arabs would allow the Jews to establish a nation there. By now, I knew that atheism and materialism were just as unsubstantial as the religions. All my probings led to the same conclusion—that there was some scheme within Creation, someone we call God, but He had not revealed Himself to anyone nor was there even the slightest indication that He desired love, peace, and justice. The whole history of man and beast; all the facts pointed to the very opposite—that this was a God of strength and cruelty Whose principle was: Might makes right.

Oddly enough, this total skepticism or agnosticism led me to a kind of private mysticism. Since God was completely unknown and eternally silent, He could be endowed with whatever traits one elected to hang upon Him. Spinoza had bestowed Him with two known attributes and an endless array of unknown ones. But why couldn't one fantasize many other attributes? Why couldn't creativeness be one of His attributes? Why couldn't beauty, harmony, growth, expediency, playfulness, humor, will, sex, change, freedom, and caprice represent divine attributes too? And where was it written that He was the only God? Maybe He belonged to a whole army of gods, an infinite hierarchy. Maybe He procreated and multiplied and brought forth billions of angels, seraphim, Aralim, and cherubim in His cosmic harem as well as new generations of gods. Since nothing was known about Him and nothing could be known, why not confer upon this divine X all the possible values? The cabalists had done this in their own fashion, the idolators in another, and the Christians and Muslims in another still. I personally was fully prepared to crown Him with all kinds of possible attributes except benevolence and compassion. To ascribe mercy to a God who for millions of years had witnessed massacres and tortures and who had literally built an entire world on the principle of violence and murder was something my sense of justice wouldn't allow me to do. In my mind I created a kind of pecking order between us. I, a dust speck trembling with fear and filled with a sort of sense of right based upon my own silly urges and convictions; He, a universal murderer, a cosmic Genghis Khan or Napoleon—eternal, infinite, omnipotent, so wise and mighty in knowledge and technique that He could keep track of every electron, every atom, every gnat, fly, and microbe. It was even possible that one could phone Him directly with a request through the medium of prayer but with no guarantee whatsoever of an answer. I had actually appropriated Spinoza's God but I had extended Him, anthropomorphized Him, bestialized Him, and reworked Him in my imagination to suit my moods. Incredibly enough, I "phoned" Him my requests and hoped somehow that He *could* answer me if the notion struck Him to do so. At that time my most urgent request was that my stories be printed and that I could have a room of my own. Being together with Gina had begun to grow tiresome for me.

Why? Because Gina grew ever more attached to me. She had seriously begun to demand that I marry her. She had grown jealous. She wanted to build her whole life upon me and even hoped that in time I would support her. I had no yen whatsoever to take a wife at least twenty years older and one that had already gone through who knows how many husbands and lovers before me. I didn't want to assume any burdens. Somehow, almost overnight, Gina had turned solemn. I no longer dared remind her of her past and she began to deny the affairs of which she had once told me. She now nagged at me to work and to be disciplined. In short, she became that which I didn't want—a wife.

3.

Again I went around looking for a place to live. Again I climbed stairs and temporarily intruded into the lives of those who wanted to give up a portion of their living quarters.

Most of the advertisements read: "For a gentleman only." Others frankly specified that the lodger must be a bachelor. Those who rented rooms were nearly all women. I rang, they opened, and we contemplated each other. After a while they asked what I did and when I told them that I worked for a publication they were instantly won over. Our glances met and mutely asked: perhaps? I had become a connoisseur of faces, bosoms, shoulders, bellies, hips. I speculated how much pleasure these various parts could provide if it came to an intimacy. At times, within the space of a few minutes I gained insight into a life. Men had died leaving widows. The rich had grown impoverished. Husbands had stayed on in Russia, fallen at the front, gone off to America, or run away with other women. For a while it would appear that fate had steered me to the right place but soon the problems would begin to emerge—the rent was too high or the room was half-dark. Some of the rooms had no stoves to heat them. Actually I couldn't afford even the cheapest room but if I was going to write I needed a room of my own. My publisher had promised to get me to do Yiddish translations of German, Polish, and Hebrew. Even as I talked to these women I formed conceptions of their character and intelligence. Some pouted and grew sarcastic when they heard that I wrote in Yiddish. Others asked if there really was such a thing as Yiddish literature. They had apparently never heard of Sholem Aleichem or Peretz, or they only made believe so. Those that agreed to rent to me for a small sum were ugly, neglected, with a houseful of children and rooms that stank of pesticide. Their kitchens exuded the smell of onions, garlic, washing soda. To go to the toilet one had to pass through the living room. My eyes wearied of looking at closets, chairs, rugs, credenzas, beds, sofas, wall clocks, samovars, portraits, and knickknacks dating back to King Sobieski's time. I inhaled the scent of perfumes, soaps, bodies. If I could have afforded a hundred zlotys a month I might have picked and chosen, but I couldn't even consider paying more than fifty.

I had written down many addresses, telephone numbers, and prices in my notebook but I hadn't found what I

wanted. It was late in spring but the weather was cold and damp. I left the last apartment of the day and my brain felt dulled from all the talk, all the impressions, and maybe even from hunger since I hadn't eaten any lunch. I hadn't yet told Gina that I was leaving and I had to make up some lie to cover my whereabouts all day. I walked down half-dark streets and I wasn't sure where I was. I glanced up at illuminated windows. Other people had somehow managed to settle in, to eat dinner with their families, and to hold down more-or-less stable jobs but I roamed through the wet city like a phantom. I had awakened that morning with plans for a novel, for stories or even a play, but it had all evaporated. Night had fallen. A deep melancholy settled over me.

I smelled the waste that was carried out from the refuse bins in the evenings and I inhaled the aromas of trees, blossoms, and turned-over soil. I passed a house gate where streetwalkers lurked calling out to passers-by. Certainly it would be crazy, having Gina, to go with one of them and risk venereal disease. I barely had enough in my pocket to pay for a meal if I decided to eat out. But somehow, my pace slowed. I was seized by a desire for a strange body, for unheard words spoken by a different voice. "Why fear syphilis?" a voice within me asked. "You're not long for this world anyhow."

I stood there and beneath the shine of the gas street lights examined the live ware. One was small and thin with

a narrow face, sunken cheeks and big black eyes that exuded a Jewish fear as if she had just escaped a pogrom or
had skipped over the few hundred years from Chmiel-
nicki's massacres. She was huddled in a shawl of a type
rarely seen in Warsaw. She looked straight at me and her
glance seemed to say: "You're the only one who can drag
me out of this mire into which I have fallen."

The second was tall, stout, wearing a yellow dress and
green boots. Her hair was as red as fire. A man had stopped
near her and seemed to be bickering with her about something but she apparently had no patience for him and
looked away. This was probably not a patron who used a
girl and paid her, but some pest who came just to gab or to
try to get something for nothing. In one hand he held a box
of the kind laborers sometimes carry to factories or work-
shops. The red-haired whore had spotted me and she
winked to me to save her from the pest. She even amiably
showed me the tip of her tongue.

A third stood off in a corner not looking at anything. Her
face was red from rouge or perhaps she had rubbed it with
red paper. I had the feeling that she neither wanted to nor
was able to compete with the others. She was obviously
waiting patiently till the other two were engaged and her
turn came.

I could decide neither to choose one of them nor to keep
going. What I now felt wasn't lust but an urge to demean
myself, to convince myself once and for all that all my

hopes were for naught and that I was already at the end of my road. "If you catch syphilis," my inner enemy went on, "you'll have to commit suicide and that will put an end to all the foolishness."

My feet crossed the street as if of their own accord. I had intended to take another one but instead I went over to the skinny one with the frightened eyes. She trembled.

"Me?"

"Yes, you."

She cast a glance at the redhead which expressed both surprise and something akin to triumph. She ducked inside the dark gate archway and I followed—"like a sheep to slaughter," I told myself. Only yesterday I had concluded that man's resemblance to God lay in the fact that both possessed freedom of choice, each in his own fashion and according to his ability. But here I was doing something that mocked all my ideas. The girl walked down stairs and I found myself in a hallway so narrow only one person could pass at a time. Blackened walls loomed heavily on either side ready to come together and crush me. The floor was bumpy and pitted. A smell of earth, rot, and something moldy and greasy assailed my nostrils. Suddenly in the shine of a tiny kerosene lamp a hugh individual with a black patch instead of a nose, a face pocked as a grater, and dressed in rags, materialized. His yellow eyes reflected the laughter of those who have looked down into the abyss and found it less frightening than comical. He walked with a waddle and blocked our path. He stank like a carcass. I started to run backward and my ears rang as if from bells tolling. My mouth filled with nauseating bile. The whore shouted and tried to run after me. The giant began to bellow, guffaw, clap his paws. I groped for the stairs but they had vanished. I heard a meowing of cats and the muffled sounds of an accordian.

"God in heaven, save me!" the believer within me cried.

I turned around and the stairs emerged. I raced up them and in a moment was outside again. The red-haired whore shrieked words I only deciphered later:

"Fool, cheat, dead beat! . . ."

It was all like a nightmare or one of those trials by Satan described in holy volumes or storybooks. I had intended to surrender myself to the powers of evil but the forces that rule the world had interfered. I was drenched with sweat. My heart pounded and my throat was parched. I was overcome by a deep feeling of shame and the silence of one who has just extricated himself from mortal danger. I prayed to the God with Whom I waged war to forgive me. I vowed never to defy Him again.

4.

I had found what I had been looking for—a room with an old couple on Dzika Street, part of which the Warsaw City Council now called Zamenhof Street after the creator of Esperanto. The owner of the apartment, Dr. Alpert, an eye doctor, had actually been a friend of the late Dr. Zamenhof, who had lived and practiced two houses away. I had studied Esperanto in Bilgoray. I had even tried writing a sketch in this international language and I considered it an honor to live at the home of a colleague of its creator. Although I had sinned, Providence had granted me what I wanted—a clean room, not expensive, decently furnished, sunny, with a window overlooking the street, and located on the fourth floor so that the outside noises weren't too disturbing. I realize now that the couple wasn't as old as they seemed to me at the time. They had a son of twenty-three or four but Dr. Alpert was completely gray and toothless, and spoke in the thin voice of an old man. He was small, stooped, had a weak heart and a half-dozen other ailments. He no longer had any connections with a hospital, and few patients came to see him. Those who did were all poor and paid according to their means. From time to time the doctor himself became sick and had to be taken to a hospital. His dull eyes beneath the bristly white eyebrows exuded the tranquillity of those who have given up all ambition and have accepted the coming of death.

Husband and wife both spoke Polish even though they

knew Yiddish. Mrs. Alpert was younger than her husband, no taller than he, with hair that had begun to thin, a pointy chin that sprouted a gray womanly beard, and brown eyes that expressed all the worries and suspicions burdened spirits carry from cradle to grave. From the very first moment she opened the door to me, she appeared frightened. She measured me sidelong, inquisitively, and began questioning me before she even allowed me inside the foyer. She told me quite frankly: Although she could have used the extra money toward the rent, she had seldom taken in a roomer. What could you know about a stranger anyway? He might be a thief, a murderer, a swindler. He might also be a Communist, an anarchist, or a syphilitic. You read of so many terrible things in the paper that no matter how careful you were, you could still fall into a net. Under no circumstance would she take in a woman lodger. Women wanted to wash out their stockings and underwear, to cook themselves meals in the kitchen. They also began to take an instant hand in the running of the household. I assured Mrs. Alpert that I wouldn't wash or cook anything, merely sit at my table and write.

After an extended interview she asked me into the living room and also showed me the doctor's reception room, the kitchen, and even her bedroom. Everything was old but clean. I needed but one glance at the son, Edek, to tell that he was sickly. He was tall, lean, and pale as a consumptive, with a high forehead, a long neck, narrow shoulders, a

sunken chest, a crooked nose, and bulging eyes. His arms were as thin as sticks. He listened to his mother's talk and made no response. From time to time he coughed. A whole stack of newspapers and magazines lay before him on a table and I noticed that they were all old and creased. Articles or ads had been clipped out of some. A scissors lay on top of the pile just like on an editor's desk.

The maid, Marila, had a high bosom and round hips. Her calves were broad and muscular, her pale blue eyes exuded a peasant strength. Mrs. Alpert introduced us and said that if I ever needed anything, a glass of tea, breakfast, or whatever, Marila was always at my service. She would make up my bed, sweep up, and keep the room in order. The girl nodded and smiled showing a mouthful of wide teeth, and dimples.

When Gina heard that I was moving out, she became hysterical. She screamed, wept, tore the hair from her head, and swore that she would take poison, hang herself, or throw herself under a streetcar. She warned me that in the other world, where she was heading, she would kneel before the Throne of Glory and tell the Almighty all the evil I had perpetrated down here on earth. She assured me that the punishment was imminent both for me and for the woman who was snatching me from her. I took a solemn oath that there was no one and that my reason for moving was so that I could work in peace, but Gina whined:

"It's true that I'm a fool but I'm not the dunce you take

me for. You found a younger and maybe a prettier one than me, but I gave you my heart and soul, and she, that whore —may she burn like fire, Dear Father in heaven—will only give you what you can get for two zlotys on Smocza Street. The trouble with men is that they don't know the difference. They're all a bunch of damn idiots, dullards, madmen, low-lifes—down to the very last one. Mama of mine, look what they're doing to me! Sainted Grandmother, come and take me to you! I can no longer stand so much shame and anguish. I'll be with you, Grandma, and with all the holy women. This phony world disgusts me. Oy, I have to vomit!"

And she dashed into the toilet where I heard her retch, cry, and like Job, curse the day she had been born. After a while it became unnaturally quiet in there. I began to pound on the door but she didn't answer. I tried to break the door down but the lock or the chain wouldn't give.

I cried: "Gina, come out! I'll stay. I'll stay with you as long as I live! I swear on all that is holy!"

The door swung open.

"Beast, don't swear! Take your bundle and go. I don't want you here any more. Oy, Holy Father of mine!"

And she went back into the toilet and resumed throwing up.

When Gina came out again I got the strange feeling that she had suddenly aged. This wasn't Gina but someone else perhaps ten years older, sallow, with bags under eyes grown dimmed and an expression about the mouth I had never seen on her. A bitterness hovered about her lips and something akin to mockery over her own ill fortune. For the first time I grasped the fact that love was no game. Love killed people. Again and again I offered to stay with her, but she said:

"No, my dearest, you are just beginning and I'm on the verge of closing the book forever."

3

The revived Polish nation was barely seven years old, but within that short time it had already gone through a war with the bolsheviks, an assassination of a president, and a great number of political crises. One spring day as I sat in my room trying to write a story, the door opened and Mrs. Alpert came in. She appeared more frightened than usual.

She said, "You sit there and write and outside a revolution has broken out."

"What kind of revolution?"

I expected to hear that the Communists were about to do to Poland what Lenin, Kamenev, Zinoviev, and Stalin had promised to do to all Europe, but Mrs. Alpert replied: "Pilsudski has taken over the power."

I had been prepared to toss my manuscript in the basket and run to wherever my legs would carry me, since the Communist hacks at the Writers Club had all assured me that when the Revolution came, they would hang me from "the nearest lamppost" along with all the rabbis, priests, members of the Polish Socialist party, Zionists, Bundists, Poale Zionists both the right and the left, and all other

counterrevolutionaries. But I had nothing to fear from Pilsudski. The party politicians at the Polish parliament, the Sejm, had forgotten that Pilsudski had established the new Poland and they ignored him. Every few weeks a new government crisis erupted. All poetic hopes that a liberated Poland would bring with it new spiritual values and a Messianic spirit for all mankind had been dashed. Now it appeared that the army with Pilsudski at its head would set up a dictatorship. For Jews in general, and for someone like me in particular, this would make no difference whatsoever. I had read somewhere that Pilsudski had criticized the Polish Ministry of War for allowing the conscription of inept and unfit recruits. I was scheduled to go before a military commission again and it occurred to me that this revolution might somehow help me avoid the draft.

It happened like this. My brother had persuaded the Palestine Bureau in Warsaw to issue me a certificate of immigration to Palestine, but since such a certificate was good for a whole family, the office made a stipulation that I marry first—whether actually or in name only. This meant going through a ceremony with a girl in Warsaw, then getting a divorce once in Palestine. Such counterfeit marriages were a frequent occurrence those days. They served to bring more Jews to the Land of Israel and also helped poor pioneers who couldn't afford the fare. The alleged "wife" would pay the travel expenses for herself and for her "husband." The whole thing smacked of fraud but Poland wanted to get rid of Jews and England didn't care if a few more Jews settled in Palestine. A large number of those that immigrated suffered disappointment, unable to adjust to the climate and the hard work, and after a while they turned back to either Poland or wherever they were admitted.

There couldn't be even the slightest thought of my getting married for real. I had read Otto Weininger's *Sex and Character* and had resolved never to marry. Weininger, Schopenhauer, Nietzsche, and my own experiences had transformed me into an antifeminist. I lusted after women yet at the same time I saw their faults, chief of which was that they (the modern, not the old-fashioned kind) were amazingly like me—just as lecherous, deceitful, egotistical, and eager for adventures. Some frankly declared that marriage was an outdated institution. How could you make a contract to love for an entire lifetime? they asked. What could be a greater contradiction than love and a contract? The novels these girls read, the magazine articles, the plays they saw, all mocked the husband who worked hard, raised his children and was deceived, and at the same time they glorified the lover who got everything for free. My experiences with Gina and with those that I met later only confirmed this conviction. Well, and what about the things I observed at the Writers Club! In my own writings the husband emerged an object of scorn.

Even a marriage in name only frightened me somewhat.

What would I do if the girl changed her mind later and refused to divorce me. I was ashamed to accept money from a woman. I didn't know where to find such a woman in the first place. My shyness was apparently obvious to the people at the Palestine Bureau, and one of the officials there recommended a girl who was ready to go through such a clandestine marriage. He told me about her in detail. She was engaged to an engineer in Warsaw, a graduate of the Warsaw Polytechnic Institute, and the wedding had been imminent when the fiancé committed some folly and was forced to flee Poland. After long wanderings he had illegally entered Palestine but he wasn't able to bring his fiancée over. Panna (Miss) Stefa came from an affluent home and was deeply in love with her fiancé. She had already met several youths with certificates of immigration but one promptly fell in love with her and urged her to enter into a real marriage with him; a second changed his mind about the whole thing since he had a girl of his own who had somehow managed to scrape together the fare for them both; and a third had tried to swindle money out of her. Miss Stefa had grown so despondent that she had given up on the entire notion. The official urged me:

"Above all, you have to convince her that you have no ulterior motives. I'll call her right now. Her father was once a very rich man but Grabski ruined him with the taxes. The daughter studied at the university, knows languages, and who knows what else."

Everything happened quickly. The official telephoned and apparently spoke well of me, for Miss Stefa asked that I come right over. I told the official that I would like to shave first and put on a better suit but he argued that the more shabby I appeared, the better my chances would be. Miss Stefa's parents lived on Leszno Street in a house built in 1913 just before the war. It had an elevator and all the modern conveniences. The official spoke of this Miss Stefa with such high regard that I was overcome with childish fear and shame at the prospect of meeting her.

Although I didn't walk quickly, I became drenched in sweat. I had knotted my shoelaces but after each few steps they came untied as if by some unseen hand. As usual whenever I grew embarrassed, the imps began to toy with me. I sneezed and my collar button fell off. I searched for it on the sidewalk but it had vanished. A button popped off my overcoat. I suddenly noticed that my trousers were hanging loosely and trailing. I tried to hitch up my suspenders but the loop holding up the trousers had snapped. I tried to apply self-hypnosis à la Coué, told myself to be bold and not allow myself to be cowed by some female no matter how rich or educated she might be, but to no avail. Crossing the street I was nearly run down by a droshky. I walked past a store front with a mirror and caught a glimpse of myself. I looked pale, drained, disheveled. I walked inside the building gate where the janitor was

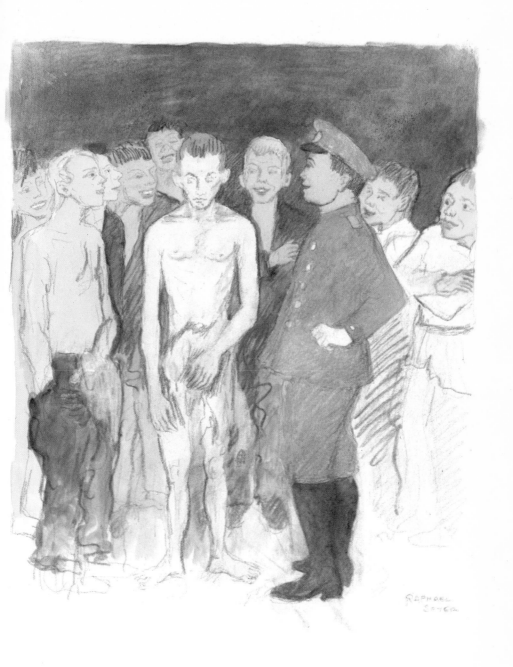

lounging. When I told him whom I wanted to visit he measured me arrogantly and asked:

"For what purpose?"

I didn't know how to answer him and he snarled through clenched teeth:

"Best get out of here! . . ."

2.

After a while I got permission to go up and I began to climb the stairs because the elevator was for tenants only. The steps were of marble. I stopped before a massive carved door painted red. A brass name plate bore the inscription: Isidore Janovsky.

I rang and it took awhile for the maid, a woman with a red face and white hair, to answer. The foyer was big and wide with many doors leading from it. The maid went off to announce me and I had to wait a long time. There wasn't a stick of furniture in the foyer. The walls bore traces of removed paintings like in a vacated apartment. A chain used to hold a lamp hung from the ceiling, but without a lamp. I suddenly recalled the official's comments that Grabski had brought Miss Stefa's father to ruin. Grabski was the Minister of Finance who had imposed such taxes upon the Jews that they were unable to pay, and after a while a wagon or wagons would come from the tax collector's office and remove all the householder's belongings. These wagons had been nicknamed "hearses."

A door opened abruptly and Miss Stefa came out. She wore a knee-length dress and her blond hair cut boyishly short. She was tall for a woman, light-skinned and snub-nosed, and her face had the expression of one who is deeply preoccupied and had been called away from an important task. She looked me up and down and asked:

"Were you sent here by the Palestine Bureau?"

"Yes, the Bureau."

She glanced at the slip of paper which I handed to her and pronounced my Jewish name in a Polish accent.

She asked: "Have you a birth certificate? A passport? Are you registered here in Warsaw? Are you ready to go to Palestine in the next few weeks? Are you deferred from conscription?"

I answered all her questions briefly. She stood away from me as if anxious to get the whole interrogation over with right then and there. Her gaze was stern and it occurred to me that she behaved not unlike those bureaucrats who had ruined her father.

After a while, she asked: "Is it true you write in the jargon?"

Her calling Yiddish a jargon irked me. Usually in such cases I would try to impress upon the other that all languages had been so disdained at first. French, Italian, and English had been branded as the vulgar languages of the

rabble while the upper classes had employed Latin. I would
point out that as long as the language of the aristocracy in
Russia and Poland had been French, the Poles and Russians hadn't produced a single work of art in that language.
But as soon as they started writing in Russian or Polish,
there had emerged a Pushkin, a Mickiewicz, a Slowacki,
and many others. But I simply replied:

"Yes, in the jargon."

"What do you write about?"

"Oh, about Jewish life here in Poland."

"And what do you intend to do in Palestine? Also
write?"

"If they'll let me."

"Do you know Hebrew?"

"I can read it and write it, but not speak it fluently. I've
never spoken any Hebrew."

"When I was a child, a rabbi used to come to the house
and teach me a little Hebrew—how to read from a prayer
book—what is it called? 'I give thanks.' But I've forgotten
everything. I no longer even know the alphabet. Such
strange characters—they all look alike to me. Well, and the
reading from right to left is bewildering. I'm afraid I'll
never get used to it. But it has turned out so that I must get
to Palestine. Come in. Why do you stand there in the door-
way?"

She opened the door for me and I followed her into a
room which contained a folding cot, a small table on which

a few books and papers lay, and two kitchen chairs—one white, one blue.

She looked around as if she herself were startled by the changes wrought here. She indicated to me to take one of the chairs while she herself sat down on the cot, which was covered with a faded bedspread. She lit a cigarette, crossed her legs, and it struck me that her knees weren't round as most girls', but pointed.

She asked: "That young man—what's his name? Margolis—explained the situation to you?"

"Yes, more or less."

"I must get to Palestine and the sooner the better. My fiancé and I were supposed to get married here in Warsaw. Everything was already set for the wedding when suddenly something happened that spoiled our plans. The Palestine Bureau won't issue a certificate for a single person. They generally discriminate against the so-called weaker sex. In this respect, they are full-fledged Asiatics."

She went on. "I know languages—French, German, even a little English, but I know no Yiddish and not a word of Hebrew. I'll be frank with you, but don't tell Margolis —I have no intention of staying in Palestine for long. Margolis is a fervent Zionist. If it were up to him, every Jew in the world would pack his bag and head for Palestine. When it comes to Poland, he may well be right. But Poland isn't the world. What will the Jews do there? It's still half desert. You're undoubtedly a Jewish nationalist, but to me the whole Jewishness is a paradox. What does my Jewishness consist of? I don't believe even marginally in God or all those miracles described in the Old Testament. I haven't the slightest notion of what's in the Talmud and all the rest of it. I was raised in the European culture but the World War has stirred up a kind of nationalism—that is beyond me. No, I don't want to stay there but it's hard to get a visa to a European country, and America has closed her gates. You've certainly read about what's going on in Russia. Did you say you were free of your military obligations?"

"I've been given a 'B' classification. I have to present myself again in a few months."

Miss Stefa snatched the cigarette from her lips and crushed it in the ashtray on the table.

"Oh really? But according to Margolis you were freed for good."

"No. He knew I must present myself again shortly."

"Has he lost his mind or what? Already he has sent me three or four candidates and each turns out worse than the last. I'm really beginning to suspect he's acting out of spite. But why would he? What are your chances of being rejected?"

"I hope they won't take me; I'm not altogether well."

"What's wrong with you?"

I wanted to say something but the words wouldn't leave

my lips. Miss Stefa measured me with a sidelong, mocking gaze.

"You don't want to go in the army, that's all. Not that I blame you. I wouldn't want to myself if I were a man. What kind of pleasure is it? But someone has to defend the country in case of attack. My fiancé, Mark, is Jewish but he served in the army and worked his way up to officer. He fought in the war against the Bolsheviks and was highly decorated. He is an outstanding horseman and marksman. He once took part in a military horse race and he received a commendation. Were you born in Poland?"

"Yes, in Poland."

"Your pronunciation sounds foreign. The Polish-Jewish press keeps fighting anti-Semitism but the Jews here behave in such a way that the anti-Semitism must exit. Thank God not all Jews are like this. You were undoubtedly raised in the heder and in the Yeshivah, on those ancient, moldy volumes. I believe you when you say you feel sick, but it's only because you've never breathed any fresh air and never done any physical labor. You're barely twenty-one or two but your spine is bent like an old man's. Why are you so pale? Are you anemic?"

"Yes. Maybe."

"What does your father do?"

"He's a rabbi."

"A rabbi, eh? Every third Jew is a rabbi. They walk the streets in their long caftans, disheveled beards, and flying earlocks and when I see them and their wild gestures I'm ashamed that we share a heritage. They are total savages."

"You're wrong, Miss Stefa, they are highly civilized."

"In what sense?"

"They want to live, not to be heroes. What the Christians merely preach, they have been practicing for two thousand years."

"Oh, you're a strange young man. I'm beginning to believe that this Margolis from the Palestine Bureau is having fun at my expense. You know what? Since you're here you can show me the Hebrew alphabet. At least I'll be able to read a sign when I am there. Wait, I have a Hebrew book. I left it in the living room. I'll be right back."

3.

From the way Miss Stefa spoke I gathered that her parents were thoroughly assimilated, but a moment after she left, the door opened and in minced a tiny individual with a minuscule white goatee and brown eyes smiling with Jewish familiarity. He had a pinched, hooked nose, a high forehead as wrinkled as parchment, and sunken cheeks. He wore a stiff collar and a black silk tie.

He said: "I hope I am not disturbing you. I am Isidore Janovsky, Stefa's father."

He spoke Polish in the very same accent as I. He smiled, revealing a mouthful of yellow teeth. I hurried to say that

R.S.

he was in his own house and that it was my pleasure to meet him, but Isidore Janovsky countered in singsong:

"What's the big pleasure? These days a father is no authority. There has grown up a generation that's ashamed of its own parents. You're undoubtedly one of the bridegrooms Margolis from the Palestine Bureau keeps sending us. Forgive me, I don't mean to sound insulting. Since my daughter has elected to drop everything and go to Palestine, she has to go through all this. There is a saying: 'Once you say A, you must also say B.' But who told her to say 'A' in the first place? . . . So, you're actually going to the Land of Israel? What will you do there? You have to work hard there and the climate is harsh. I'm not just talking through my hat—I've been there. I visited the colonies and all the rest of it. Before the war I was a rich man and could afford to travel. When it gets hot there and the chamsin starts blowing you can go mad. I became very sick there. The colonies, Rishon le Zion and Petah Tikvah, are certainly an accomplishment, but outside of the piece of bread they provide nothing, and when the crops are meager they don't even provide that. The Zionists claim things are better now —but I'm no heretic if I choose not to believe them. At one time a lie was a lie. Today, they've given the lie a fancy name—propaganda. May I ask your profession?"

"I'm a proofreader for a literary magazine."

Isidore Janovsky clapped his ear.

"From this you make a living?"

"Yes."

"And what will you do in the Land of Israel? Be a proofreader too? What's the name of the magazine? What is it in—Hebrew or jargon?"

"In Yiddish."

"Over there they look down on Yiddish. My dear young man, since you're a proofreader you are probably something of a writer too. I used to read the older writers—Mendele, Sholem Aleichem, Peretz, Dinesohn. It had a kind of flavor. Once, one of the current crop of writers gave me his book. I didn't understand a single line. Such difficult words and one had no connection to the next. They're all Communists. In Russia it's hell—people are starving to death and if one utters a word against their rulers they send him to Siberia. Here it's bitter too. Without the Russian market Poland is like a head without a body. They want their taxes paid but how can you pay taxes when the factories have no customers to supply? What's the name of that magazine?"

I told him its name.

"Never heard of it. I shouldn't say this to you but I'm going to say it anyway. We have one daughter who is very precious to us. There was another, a younger, a girl of seventeen, wonderful child—pretty, smart, devoted to her parents, a treasure, but she got the crazy urge to dance. She danced and danced till her appendix burst and before the doctors, those quacks, could diagnose her ailment it was too late. It's no tragedy when a girl dances but everything has to have a limit. There has evolved a generation that knows no restraints. They want to drink in all the pleasure all at once, and if you tell them that this isn't the way, they're ready to tear you to shreds. Anyhow, she passed on and took our hearts with her. It almost killed her mother. Her every moment is torture. How she goes on living is one of God's miracles. I say this in connection with the fact that Stefa—her real name is Sheba Leah—is all we've got left now. Once she leaves, her mother won't last a month. The story is this: If she were only going to someone worthy of her, it would be at least some consolation for me. It's accepted that a daughter has to be given away. We wouldn't want her to remain an old maid, God forbid. Maybe we would even follow her to Palestine or wherever she might settle. But she's mixed up with the worst charlatan in Warsaw. To begin with, he had a wife who refused to divorce him and it cost a fortune to buy her off. He had a rich father who left him a large inheritance but he, Mark, lost it all. Yes, he literally gambled it away at cards, roulette, and other such games whose names I don't even know. He has a gambling mania. He'll bet on anything and he hasn't won a bet yet. I discussed this with a doctor, a psychiatrist, and he told me that this is a sickness. He must constantly be risking something. He became a regular big shot in the Polish Army, a real hero. Each time they needed someone for a dangerous job he was the first to volunteer. He has jumped horses over fences and he has already killed several of them. It was a miracle he didn't kill himself or become crippled. How a Jew could be born so reckless is beyond me. Such lunatics existed among the old Polish gentry. They would risk their fortune on the turn of a card or in lawsuits that dragged on for years and bankrupted both the litigants. I didn't know his father, he died during the war, but he has an old bitch of a mother who is just as crazy as he is. She was left a lot of money but her son got it away from her, although they say she still has a bundle salted away somewhere. She never leaves her house since she lives in constant fright of thieves. He, that Mark, had to flee Poland because—"

The door opened and Stefa appeared holding a book.

"So, Papa, you're baring your soul to him? You're confessing already? The moment a person walks into the house he assails him with his tales of misery. Papa, if you ever again—"

"Hush, daughter, hush, I'm not doing anything to harm you. Believe me, you don't have a better friend than me. . . ."

"God protect me from such friends."

"You should be ashamed to talk this way to your father, daughter. We gave our lives for you and look how you repay us."

"What am I doing to you, Papa? What harm am I causing you? I love someone and I want to be with him. Is that such a crime?"

"You know very well that your going to Palestine thousands of miles away will finish your mother. About me, you needn't worry. I've lived long enough as it is. What else can life offer me—that the 'hearse' come again and snatch the pillow from under my head? But I can't stand to watch your mother suffering and I feel for you too, daughter, because the man you're going to will—"

"Papa, be quiet!"

4.

Isidore Janovsky went out and Stefa said:

"He's my father and I love him but he is an exhibitionist. He likes to bare all wounds and not only his own but my mother's, mine, and everybody else's as well. Is this a specifically Jewish condition? Why deny it? We're a shattered family in every respect, but we aren't yet beggars to display all our sores in public. Show me the alphabet and how to read it."

Stefa opened the book and I showed her the alphabet.

She interrupted to complain: "Why did they make the *nun* and *gimel* so much alike? Also the *mem* and the *tet* . . . and the *daled* and the *resh*? I can't understand this. It's the same in the Gothic script too. In English, on the other hand, you never know how a word should be pronounced. In Hebrew it's even worse. I was already reading Hebrew, but I've forgotten it. I'm beginning to believe that those who developed scripts and languages were all idiots. I'd like to hide on some island without culture and languages and live like a bird or an animal. But where do you find such an island? Is there really such a thing as Yiddish literature?"

"Yes, there is."

"What is it?"

"A literature like all the others—ninety-nine per cent bad and one per cent good."

"You're a funny young man—you speak the truth. I've turned into a half anti-Semite. I can't stand Jews. They're always running, bustling, mouthing endless complaints against everyone and only striving to create a better world. Mark is that way too. I love him, yet I see all his faults. Why am I telling you these things? I never talk to anyone, but since you are a writer—or wish to be a writer—you should possess some understanding. My father undoubtedly blabbed everything to you. He does this with whoever comes into the house, even the man who collects the money from the gas meter. Let's read on."

We resumed and it didn't take Stefa more than fifteen minutes to begin reading faultlessly. She had already gone through this book with someone else before. She read and smoked. She even remembered the meaning of some of the words. She read to the bottom of a page and said:

"You lack strength because you don't eat. It's just that simple, and you don't eat because you don't want to be conscripted. But that won't help you. The doctors are on to these tricks. When they classify a person 'B', it means he is organically sound. Why can't you smuggle yourself across into Germany or Rumania and catch a ship from there to Palestine?"

"I don't know how to go about this."

Stefa closed the book.

"Listen to me. I must depart as soon as possible. I can't put things off for the future. My fiancé is waiting for me with impatience. Neither can I stay away from him. Each day without him is for me like hell. According to the letters with which he showers me, he yearns for me too. My father probably managed to malign him, but he is the most interesting person I've ever met. I have the exact amount needed to pay the fare for two people. We must get to Constantsa and board a ship there. That's the cheapest route. I have everything figured down to the very last groschen. If they get the notion to raise the fare, it's all over for us. We have relatives and so-called friends here, but no one can nor wants to help us. What did Father say about Mark?"

"Nothing bad. Only that he likes to gamble and take risks."

"Yes, that's one of his aberrations. Do you at least have a domestic passport?"

"I don't even have a birth certificate."

"We can go to Danzig. You don't need a foreign passport to go there since it's a free city. No, that wouldn't do. It's too far from there to Rumania. We must go to Zaleszczyki in Galicia and from there cross on foot into Rumania. There are smugglers everywhere who will guide you across the border for a few zlotys."

"They wouldn't let me aboard ship without a foreign passport. I couldn't get the certificate without it either," I said.

"What? A regular foreign passport costs four hundred zlotys. To receive a concession on this price you have to present all kinds of petitions, and the *starosta* and the government commissariat set up delays and obstacles. They might even levy taxes against you or at least demand proof that you don't owe any. Do you have such proof?"

"I have nothing."

"You have nothing. . . . Where do you live anyway—on the moon?"

"I wish I could."

"Well, I see how things are. Margolis only sends me young men to waste my time so that it will all come to naught. He is my enemy but I don't know why. Are you hungry?"

"Hungry? No."

"You look hungry. I don't want you to pass out in my room. I know of a young man who starved himself for so long that he dropped dead. We have a maid; that one who let you in. But we can't pay her a salary so she has become like the mistress of the house. If she feels like it, she cooks, if she doesn't, we eat dry food. She's been with us since I remember and she's like part of the family. She adored my younger sister but she spites me at every turn. My sister is dead."

"Yes, I know."

"So he told you everything, the old chatterbox. Totally lacking in character. If he weren't my father I'd call him a dishrag. But I know he wasn't always like this. There are troubles that can change a person's character. Be that as it may, our maid hates visitors, particularly mine. Come, we'll go down to a café and grab a bite. I see that all my plans will come to nothing, but I do believe that your intentions are good and in my situation even a little goodwill helps. Come."

"Really, I'm not hungry."

"You'll eat, you'll eat. I won't order too much for you anyway since I must literally count every groschen. It's come to it that when I have to go somewhere, I walk to save the few groschen trolley fare."

I got up to go but at that moment there was a knock on the door. It was Isidore Janovsky. He said to Stefa:

"You're wanted on the phone."

"Who wants me?"

"Since you're wanted—go!"

"It's Treitler, eh?"

"Yes, Treitler."

"Papa, I'm not at home to him."

"Daughter, I told him you were home. Don't make me out a liar."

"I've told you countless times that I don't want to talk to him."

"Tell it to him yourself. I'm not your errand boy."

5.

There was no restaurant in the immediate neighborhood and Stefa took me to a café on the same street. She spoke to me, but she kept her face averted giving the impression that she was talking to herself.

She asked: "What kind of name is Treitler? Jews have such odd names."

"It comes from Treitle. Perhaps a German name."

"And what's the meaning of Treitle? And how is it my father is called Janovsky? It just so happened that this name came in handy when I was attending the Gymnasium, and even more so at the university. Janovsky is a true Polish name but my birth certificate lists me as Sheba Leah. These are all trifles, but one suffers because of them. When my Polish teacher pronounced the name Sheba Leah he did it with such venom, such irony! I never wanted to be Jewish, but to accept Jesus—another Jew and martyr—that wasn't to my liking either. Must people be-

long to a group and drag along all its burdens of superstition and discrimination behind them? Why can't there
be one united mankind with one language?"

"Dr. Zamenhof tried this too. I actually live on the street
named after him which used to be part of Dzika Street.
People don't want to belong to a united mankind."

"Why not? In Palestine I'll probably become Sheba
Leah again. Jewish nationalism has reared its head there.
They return to a land they left two thousand years ago.
They want to revive a language that was dead even then.
The Jews spoke Aramaic and Greek in the time of Jesus.
I've read Graetz, I've read him. I thought he would solve
the Jewish enigma for me but he himself was a fervent na-
tionalist and committed to all its dogmas. Here we are."

We had come to the restaurant. We went in, took a
table, and Stefa said:

"I'm not religious, actually, I'm an atheist, but there *is*
some hidden force that directs people's lives. It's an evil
force, not a good one. I was prettier than my sister, a better
student, taller too. She took after Papa. But the men pur-
sued her, and for some reason, ignored me. When she
lived, the telephone never stopped ringing. A day didn't go
by without her getting some invitation. She left behind
whole stacks of love letters, a regular archive. My affairs—
if they took place at all—were brief and always filled with
misunderstandings that embittered everybody. Mark came
into my life after my sister's death and I had the eerie feel-

ing that it was she who had kept the men away from me. This was silly nonsense but all kinds of crazy notions flit through one's brain. When Mark did what he did and had to flee, I got the strange feeling that my sister's ghost—or whatever you might call it—had revived after the shock of death and that she had resumed her silent war against me. Deep inside we are all rooted in the Middle Ages or maybe even in prehistoric times. This Treitler is actually the only man outside of Mark who is in love with me. But he's old enough to be my father, in his late fifties if not sixty. And I'd sooner let myself be hacked to pieces than marry him. No one has ever repelled me like he does. Nor can I understand what he sees in me. There couldn't be two more opposite types than we are. Why am I telling you all this? It's not entirely without a reason. I want a favor from you. You are my last straw."

"I am ready to do everything for you."

"Why, of all things? Because I am buying you a glass of coffee?"

"Not because of that. But—"

"It doesn't matter. Once you hear what I want, you'll have a change of heart and I'll understand. The story is this. It's already clear to me that I won't be leaving on that certificate in the near future. There were several other young men before you and each of them brought his own complications. I'm convinced that this Margolis not only doesn't want to help me but actually wants to place obstacles in my path. Even if he did want to help me, it would all be too late. I'll be perfectly honest with you—Mark left me pregnant."

Stefa uttered these last words as if in a single breath. Just then the waiter came up.

Stefa ordered two tomato soups, rolls and butter, and coffee. After the waiter left, she said:

"Oh, you can still blush. That's good. I had assumed this was no longer possible these days. You're still young. I'm five years older than you and in my case, it's as if I were twenty years older. He didn't seduce me. You might even say that I seduced him. I desperately wanted to have his child and when it became clear that he would have to flee and we might never see each other again, I demanded that he leave me his child. You probably can't understand such things because you're a male. My parents don't know a thing about it. If they ever found out it would cause a terrible row. They're so old-fashioned—you might even say backward—they could be living two centuries ago. It would kill them both as surely as it's day now. I'm not the hysterical sort but I've thought seriously about killing them both and then doing away with myself. After what they went through with my sister, I can't subject them to a new blow. I still hope that Mark and I can be reunited. Even if he came back to Poland and stood trial it wouldn't be the end of it. He didn't murder anybody, merely forged a piece of paper. Nor would I want to destroy his child. My parents still nurse hopes that I'll provide them with a half-dozen grandchildren. What they need with grandchildren only God knows. The situation of the Jews here is desperate. The Poles have had quite enough of us and I can see their side of it. We've lived here for eight hundred years and have remained strangers. Their God is not our God, their history is not our history. Most of us can't even speak a proper Polish. One time I watched a huge Zionist demonstration with blue and white flags and Stars of David and the whole falderal. They stopped the trolleys and shouted slogans in Hebrew or Yiddish. The gentiles stood around staring as if at a freak show. Just the same my parents want grandchildren. If I choose not to destroy them and myself as well, I must go through with this phony marriage ceremony regardless whether we can leave at once or must first go through the thousands of formalities. So long as I bear someone's name the humiliation won't seem as great to them. Your soup is getting cold."

"May I ask what month you are in?"

"Surely in the fourth and maybe even the fifth. Don't look so alarmed. It was I that sinned, not you."

"I'm not alarmed. . . . You're not showing at all . . . not even a trace."

"Soon it will show. I lace my corset so tightly now I can barely breathe."

4

I.

At first it seemed that Pilsudski's coup would be bloodless.
Pilsudski the marshal and Wojciechowski the president
met on some bridge, and after Pilsudski called the other a
name, Wojciechowski capitulated. That was what Mrs. Alpert had heard on the radio and that's what she had passed
along to me. But presently the shooting commenced and
news came of dead and wounded. People had already paid
with their heads or been maimed. A civil war threatened. It
was in the interests of many elements that a blood bath
erupt. The Ruthenians and White Russians who, following the Brest-Litovsk Treaty, had been left under Polish
rule awaited the opportunity to break away from Poland.
Russia had lost the war in 1920 but by now she already
possessed a strong army and she wouldn't have minded
regaining her lost territories or simply seizing all Poland
and instituting her order there. The Germans would have
been delighted to take back Upper Silesia. The Communists at the Writers Club whispered conspiratorially and
held clandestine meetings. Zinoviev and Kamenev were
plotting the world revolution. They had their functionaries

in Poland who came to the Writers Club with their direc-
tives. Nor was there a lack in Poland of those eager to
exploit this opportunity to beat Jews. I wanted to do what
Jews had done for two thousand years—flee or hide somewhere until the danger passed. But there was no place to
run or hide. My enemies were Jewish youths, fledgling
writers who lauded the Russian revolution, already
glorified Comrade Stalin, wrote odes to the Cheka and
Comrade Dzerzhinski, and demanded death for all rabbis,
priests, bourgeois, Zionists, and even Socialists who didn't
follow the Moscow line.

I was shocked to see how bloodthirsty Jewish boys and
girls had become. Two thousand years of exile, ghetto, and
Torah hadn't created a biological Jew. All it took was a few
pamphlets and speeches to erase everything the books of
morals had tried to imbue in us throughout the generations. Within me asceticism warred with the urge to give in
to all the passions. I reminded myself a hundred times a day
that all was vanity; yet a friendly girlish glance or a compli-
ment about my writing would be enough to arouse me.
This inner lack of consistency both astounded and shamed
me.

I lay in bed in my room holding a book of the sort used by
storekeepers to mark down their debts and credits and a
pencil, ready once and for all to take an accounting of the
world, to come to some firm conclusion and commence a
life based on my convictions so that my conduct could serve

as an example (or a maxim as Kant put it). On a chair nearby I had placed a history of philosophy and a number of other books which might help me restore order to my disturbed spirit. From Bresler's Library I had borrowed a collection of Tolstoy's moral stories and essays, Spinoza's *Ethics,* Kant's *Critique of Practical Understanding,* Schopenhauer's *The World as Will and Idea,* Nietzsche's *Thus Spake Zarathustra,* a book by the pacifist Forster (I've forgotten its title), Payot's *The Education of the Will,* and several books on hypnotism, autosuggestion (Coué, Charles Baudouin), and who knows what else—all of them works that touched on the essentials. I had even bought *The Path of the Righteous,* by Rabbi Moshe Haim Luzzatto, and the Book of Deuteronomy, which I had considered the wisest work ever created by man. I was ready to reappraise all values even as I heard shooting outside and was involved in an adventure that could bring me only grief.

What didn't I scribble into this account book that I had bought from a pushcart of remnants? Regimens for behavior, themes for stories, novels, plays; rules of physical and spiritual hygiene I had learned from this same Payot; all kinds of aphorisms which might have been my own or dimmed memories of something I had read and forgotten; sketches that I couldn't finish since they lacked plots; and nothing less but a rewrite of the Ten Commandments. Bits of these revised commandments (I think they grew to twelve under my direction) I still recall to this day. "Do not kill or exploit the animal, don't eat its flesh, don't flail its hide, don't force it to do things against its nature. . . ."

To "Thou shalt not kill," I added: "Control the birth of man and beast—He who said, 'Thou shalt not kill,' should have also said: 'Thou shalt not overly procreate.' . . ."

To "Thou shalt not commit adultery," I added that no marriage should last longer than fifteen years. Right next to this piece of audacity I drew a creature with the antlers of a deer, the scales and fins of a fish, and the legs of a rooster. Contemplating what I knew of history and my own nature, I had already come to the conclusion that human beings are in constant need of adventure, change, risk, danger, challenge. The fear of boredom is as great as and often greater than the fear of death. But is there a base for ethics in the face of that biological necessity? Aren't all commandments just wishful thinking? Can there be as much adventure in curbing the emotions as in letting them have their way? Can there be as much hazard in building as in destroying? Can man ever learn to indulge in the whims and excitements of his nature without hurting other people and animals? Many times I had decided that this was impossible, but I kept on returning to this problem of all problems which has been bothering me from my childhood. I still hoped against hope that science, art, technological advance, and permanent study of how to have fun without doing evil to others may replace the lust for murder, rape, treachery, revenge, and all the other destructive passions for which mankind pays such a terrible price. I was dreaming not only of a new philosophy, a new religion, a new social order, but also of new ways of amusing people and giving them the tension which they must have to be themselves.

Whole pages of the book were filled with figures. Since my job as proofreader of the literary publication wasn't secure and I was liable at any day to be left without an income, I tried to calculate the minimum amount I would need to avoid starving to death, sleeping in the streets, or asking my brother's help. Now that he had the job with the *Forward* he offered me money at every opportunity but I was resolved not to accept it. I had seen so much sponging by the young writers at the Club that I had sworn to myself never to seek help from anybody. I figured out how much starch, fat, and protein one needed to survive and how much this would cost. As for vitamins, I probably didn't know anything about them or didn't believe in them.

The net in which I entangled myself consisted of the fact that I had promised to marry Stefa, in name only, of course. Nevertheless, I intended to stand under the wedding canopy with her and even sign documents in such a way that her parents would be taken in. Thus, even if she didn't manage to make it to Palestine in time it would mean that she had a husband and a father for her child—at least to the neighbors and distant relatives. The whole scheme was insane since the child would be born some four and a half months hence and no one would be duped into believing me its father. By this time already, I realized that in moments of desperation people forsake all reason. The question merely was why I had agreed to this.

The answer was that first of all, I was desperate myself —unable to sleep nights for fear of the draft. Secondly, I somehow couldn't refuse such an elegant and educated young lady. And thirdly, I yearned for some of the suspense found in the works of Balzac, Victor Hugo, Tolstoy, Dostoevsky, Flaubert, Alexander Dumas, and Strindberg. Yiddish and Hebrew literature both suffered from a lack of suspense. Everything in them centered around some Yeshiva student who had gone astray, sought worldly knowledge, then suffered the consequences at the Yeshiva or at his in-laws'. But I had already grasped the fact that suspense was the essence of both life and art. Mere description wasn't enough. What was needed was tangled situations and genuine dilemmas and crises. A work of fiction had to draw its readers. In later years the suspense in my life and in my writing fused in such fashion that I often didn't know where one began and the other ended.

The maid, Marila, knocked on my door to announce that I was wanted on the telephone. I asked her who was calling and she countered.

"A pretty young miss."

2.

It was Gina calling. I was supposed to come to her for dinner that night and naturally, to sleep over. I was reconciled to the fact that Gina would talk about death. She often spoke in the tone of one gravely ill and whose days are numbered. I never took her words seriously since she often interspersed these conversations with plans leading months and years ahead. She intended to collaborate with me on a book, a play. I had long since perceived that talk about her death stimulated her sexually. Often in the nights she extracted my promise to attend her funeral and demanded declarations of how and with whom I would spend the time immediately following her death. She went into details that struck me as mad, but it was obvious that they aroused her desire. Even then I knew that one could not question the emotions and that the division between sanity and insanity was remarkably slender. Within every brain and nervous system lurked cells of madness and criminality. Well, but ever since I had moved out of her place I had been haunted by the suspicion that Gina was really sick. She had lost her appetite and lost weight. Her complexion had turned yellowish. She had begun to address me in a strange mixture of irony and maternal concern. She often reminded me that I had promised to say the Kaddish over her even though I had broken the laws of

Jewishness and had communicated to her my outlandish theory concerning religious protest.

Everything had grown remarkably complicated, but I needed these complications and sought others. At the Writers Club I met one of those girls who were called in jest "literary supplements." They came to the Club to partake of the literary and journalistic gossip, to strike up acquaintance with the writers and launch illicit affairs with them. At times it came out that these girls—there were some married women among them as well—wrote poems in Yiddish or in Polish. Some were Zionistically inclined and wanted to go to Palestine; others were Communist sympathizers who one day might cross illegally into the Soviet Union. Some came from wealthy families, and the literary Don Juans got small loans from them. The management of the Writers Club made frequent resolutions to bar these women. It was voted that no one but members and their wives or husbands would be admitted. A number of special guest cards were printed and a woman was stationed by the door to keep strangers out. But somehow it was impossible to get rid of these hangers-on. They claimed to love Yiddish literature, they admired the writers' talents. Some offered to translate the writers' works into Polish. Although the Yiddish actors had their own union, many actors and actresses were standing guests of the Writers Club—painters and sculptors as well as potential producers of Yiddish films who were merely waiting for the right screenplay and money. The proprietor of the buffet and the waitresses often extended credit to these uninvited guests.

Miss Sabina was small and plump, with a high bosom, a short neck, a hooked nose, full lips, and a pair of brown eyes that reflected the merriment of those who have little to hope for. She made jokes, smoked cigarettes, told spicy anecdotes. She owned a Yiddish typewriter and the writers occasionally gave her a manuscript to type. She worked in a library part-time and supported a widowed mother and two younger brothers. Sabina claimed to be my age but she looked older. She dressed poorly and with a touch of the Bohemian. Someone had told me that she had been the sweetheart of an old writer with one lung and one kidney who had been impotent besides. He had just recently died.

Sabina talked a lot and told me stories that seemed to be lies, but I subsequently became convinced that for all their strangeness they were true. The impotent old writer had had a whole harem of mistresses. He spent every penny he earned on them. He had indulged in all kinds of quirks and perversions. He slept days (after swallowing enormous quantities of sleeping pills) and stayed up nights. He had stopped writing fiction in his last years and lived from the one *feuilleton* he published every Friday. He would write the piece at the last minute, at the same time consuming so many cigarettes that once a dense smoke began issuing from his window and the policeman outside called the fire department. L. M. Preshburger, as I call him here, had lost

the talent or the urge to write, but he had concentrated all his art in his tongue. He would repose on the couch, smoke, drink, and utter words that evoked amazement, shock, and awe from his female admirers. The doctors had long since given him up—he lived in defiance of all the laws of medicine.

Sabina liked to walk while Gina had stopped taking walks since she complained of pains in her legs. Sabina would accompany me for miles. After Pilsudski became the dictator, we went to see the damaged buildings where the fighting had taken place. We bought rolls from a street vendor and munched them as we strolled along. Sabina had told me her life story in all the details. She was descended from rabbis and merchants. Her father had died of typhoid fever leaving nothing but a large apartment of six rooms plus a kitchen. Because of the rent control the rent was cheap and her mother rented rooms to elderly bachelors and cooked lunch for them. One time, the mother rented a room to a female cousin, a rabbi's daughter who turned out to be a Soviet agent. One night the house was surrounded by police, the cousin was arrested and sentenced to death. However, the Communists managed to free her and smuggled her into Russia where she became a highly placed official in some ministry and a leader in the Comintern. Beside her passion for communism, this cousin had a wild appetite for men. It later came out that she had had doings with all the old bachelors in the apartment, and following her arrest, one of them (after learning that he hadn't been her only lover) attempted suicide.

Yiddish literature had remained naïve and primitive and even its radicalism was provincial, but from Sabina's lips poured tales of high adventure. After nearly two thousand years of ghettos and extreme segregation from the gentile world, there had been awakened in the emancipated Jew an enormous yearning for worldliness coupled with a boundless energy. In Poland, this transformation had evolved later than in the other lands, but with incredible rapidity. Yiddish literature with its sentimentality and slow pace wasn't ready for such a transformation. The same writers who told astounding stories at the Writers Club trembled the moment they took pen in hand lest, God forbid, they slip into melodrama. Among the Communist writers it had become fashionable to fling mud at the *shtetl* and to contend that its time had passed. But even this they did in provincial fashion. From reading the world literature I had realized that the gentile writers too lacked the perception to describe the epoch in which they lived. They were also rooted in a literary tradition which discouraged them from writing what their eyes saw.

There had appeared such works as *Jean Christophe,* by Romain Rolland, and *The Magic Mountain,* by Thomas Mann. I had translated this latter work into Yiddish and I had had the opportunity to analyze its construction so to say "from the inside." Both these works represented long essays spiced with description. Neither Jean Christophe nor Hans Castorp were living beings but mouthpieces through which the authors spoke. Both books lacked the suspense and vitality that great literature evokes in a reader even if he is a simple soul. These were works for intellectuals seeking a purpose, a sum total, a cross section of culture, an indication for the future, and other such fine things that no art (and actually no philosophy) is capable of supplying. These were works for critics, not readers. They bored me, but I was afraid to say so since all so-called aesthetes had seized on them as if they were treasures. Already then I realized that there was emerging in the world the kind of reader who sought in a book not the synthetic but the analytical. They dissected the books they read and the deader the corpse, the more successful the autopsy. I liked much better Thomas Mann's *The Buddenbrooks* and Romain Rolland's *Colas Breugnon*, works full of the zest of life.

3.

I had written a story and submitted it to the editor of the magazine of which I was the proofreader. He promised to read it and if it pleased him, to publish it. After a while he informed me that he had read the story and even though he found it flawed, he would print it. I asked him what these flaws were and after some deliberation he said that the piece was too pessimistic, that it lacked problems, and that the story was negative and almost anti-Semitic. Why write about thieves and whores when there were so many decent Jewish men and devoted Jewish wives? If such a thing were translated into Polish and a gentile read it, he might conclude that all Jews were depraved. A Yiddish writer, my editor argued, was honor-bound to stress the good in our people, the lofty and sacred. He had to be an eloquent defender of the Jews, not their defamer.

I didn't have the opportunity to answer him since the telephone rang at that moment and he stayed on it for a long time, but his comments irked me. Why did a story have to be optimistic? What sort of criterion was this? And what did it mean that it "lacked problems"? Wasn't the essence of the existence of the world and of the human species one enormous problem? And why must a Yiddish writer be a defender of his people? Was it the Yiddish writer's obligation to conduct an eternal dialogue with the anti-Semites? Could a work written in this vein possess any artistic value? The Scriptures on which I have been raised didn't flatter the Jews. Quite the contrary, they constantly spoke of their transgressions. Even Moses didn't emerge pure. I didn't have too high an opinion of this editor and his contentions. I had observed his politicking. Now he was a Communist and now an anti-Communist. Now he was for Zionism, now against it. He published and praised bad things by known writers and often rejected good things by unknown writers. Might was right always and everywhere—in literature, in the universities, in the community office that appointed rabbis, in the Vatican, even among those who demanded justice for the exploited and oppressed. As soon as two people met, one assumed the dominant role.

In America, a faction had formed among Yiddish writers called Die Junge (The Young). In their little magazines they poured vitriol upon "the old." The Yiddish newspaper publishers in Warsaw had engaged persons of little taste to be critics. My friend Aaron Zeitlin told me that some vandal of an editor had permitted essays written by his father, Hillel Zeitlin, to be altered, cut, and often corrupted. Hillel Zeitlin was a deep thinker, a cabalist, and an exceptionally capable journalist besides. God had granted power to every bully to annoy and destroy animals and people as well. I noted with sorrow that I was no exception. In my chance opportunities to write reviews I had already denigrated writers whose works had displeased me. No matter how weak one was there was always someone weaker upon whom he might vent his fangs and claws.

I managed to do this with Gina. The more drawn she grew to me, the more drawn was I to others. Although I felt no love toward her (who knows what love is anyway), I started up with the maid at the house where I boarded. Marila and I had already kissed and made clandestine plans for me to come to her in the kitchen when the household was asleep. I had also promised to go through with the wedding ceremony with Miss Stefa, an act which Gina would consider treacherous. Stefa had sent off a long letter to her fiancé and everything depended upon his reply.

I had become a thief not for money but for love. I had discovered how easy it was to inveigle oneself into a woman's heart. I had even tried to start something with Stefa. I did it all with the quiet desperation of one who is aware of how senseless his deeds are. I often felt as if I were two people—one young, full of ambition, passion, and hope; the other a melancholic indulging in a final frolic before being lowered into the grave. Oddly enough, all the Jewish funerals wound beneath Gina's window while all the Catholic passed beneath mine on Zamenhof Street. I constantly heard the dirges of priests and sometimes, Chopin's Funeral March as well. Each time I glanced outside I caught glimpses of a coffin bedecked with garlands (real or tin), a priest in a cassock with lace at the sleeves and a miter, men carrying halberds and lanterns, and women with black-veiled faces and hats draped in crepe. The female Jewish mourners shouted their laments, clawed their cheeks, and howled in chorus while the gentiles bowed their heads silently. Death notices plastered all the walls, and the newspapers were filled with obituaries. Every second, people passed into eternity. But what was the eternity? So long as I couldn't find the answer to this, all I did was sheer futility.

Was this state of mind hypochondria or a true foreboding

of death? I often went to sleep with the certainty that I would never get up any more. When l went to buy razor blades and the storekeeper asked if I wanted two blades or five, I always answered: "Two."

I still groped in books hoping for an answer, but I knew beforehand that none would be forthcoming. I even became disappointed in psychic research. The dead who supposedly materialized at séances spoke as silly as the living. One had to be an idiot to believe in their authenticity. The philosophers' commentaries all led to the same conclusion: We neither know nor could know the essence of things. I believed in God anyhow, but there wasn't, nor probably would there ever be, any proof that He preferred Gandhi to Hitler, Stalin, or Genghis Khan.

I often heard people say: I believe in Zionism, in socialism, in a better world, in the endurance of Jews, in the power of literature, in democracy, and in many other such beliefs. But on what did they base their faiths? I could never forget the twenty million people who had perished in the war almost before my very eyes, this one for Russia, that one for Germany, some for the Revolution, others for the Counter-Revolution, this one while capturing some village, the other while retreating from the same village. Where were they, all those murderers and all those murdered? Did they share the same paradise? Were they roasting in hell together?

The telephone rang and Marila came to announce that it

was for me. She smirked and winked. I had already given her the right to be jealous. Her cheeks were red, her eyes blue. They reflected both strength and curiosity. It was Stefa calling. I barely recognized her voice. She sounded hoarse and choking, like someone gravely ill.

She said: "Something has happened. Come right over! Don't leave me waiting. When will you be here?"

"What's happened?" I asked.

"Nothing good. Come at once!"

And she hung up the receiver.

I started right off for her house. I wasn't too concerned whether the news was good or bad. I needed momentarily to forget myself with something. What could have happened? Had someone in the family taken ill? Had someone died? Hurrying along, it struck me how light I felt. From not eating I had lost weight. I would wake up in the middle of the night and my brain would be churning like a machine. I suffered from nightmares. Sometimes my fantasies evoked laughter even in myself. I had conquered not only earth but all the planets in all the galaxies. God had endowed me with powers He possibly didn't possess Himself. Through some miracle I conducted affairs with all the beauties of all the ages. Since time and space were merely points of view and even existence itself was, as Salomon Maimon and the neo-Kantians clearly brought out, a category of thinking, perhaps miracles were more real than the laws of nature. Either everything that had ever been existed or nothing existed. You could roll back time like the hands of a watch. Since the world of deed and matter was energy and perhaps spirit, all impossibilities were nothing more than temporary inhibitions. I often felt myself being transported within seconds from depression to exultation and vice versa. I consulted the psychiatric textbooks and was fully cognizant of the symptoms.

I rang Isidore Janovsky's bell and Stefa opened the door instantly, as if she had been waiting for me on the other side of the threshold. I barely recognized her. In the few days I hadn't seen her she had grown pale, emaciated, sallow. She looked disheveled, like someone who had just left her sickbed. She wore an old bathrobe and frayed slippers. She gazed at me a moment numbly as if she didn't recognize me, then seized my wrist and led me to her room. She virtually dragged me along.

Stefa's room was in disarray as if she had been packing to go on a trip. Dresses, underwear, and stockings lay scattered across the floor along with books, magazines, and papers. The bed was unmade and toothbrushes, vials of perfume, jars of salves, and toothpaste lay strewn over the sheet. For a long while Stefa stared at me with the disoriented gaze of one who primed herself to say something but has forgotten what it was she wanted to say. Finally, she blurted:

"He got married, that idiot! Ran away with some whore from England! Nothing is left me but to die!"

"How do you know this?"

"Eh? I know. I have a girl friend there and she telegraphed me. He is no longer in Palestine either. Left with her for England or the devil knows where. Maybe India."

"In that case, he is really a criminal."

"Eh? A charlatan, a madman, a scoundrel. We shared a great love but now he has killed it. It's my fault, mine! My father was right. He needed but one look at him to know what he is. But he bedazzled me, hypnotized me. Well, what's the difference? I must die and that would be a minor tragedy. That would actually be a release for me from all my misfortunes. But I simply can't pass such a blow onto my parents. They lost one daughter, and now the other? Unless I took an ax and chopped off their heads. Yes, that's it!"

"No, Miss Stefa, we are still Jews."

"Eh? What kind of Jews are we? Maybe you are a Jew but what does my Jewishness consist of? I never wanted to be one. I was as ashamed of it as if of a scurf. He, Mark, ran from it too. But after he forged that promissory note and had to flee, he ran straight to Palestine. I helped him with my money, otherwise he would be rotting in jail this very minute. He had lost forty thousand zlotys to a colonel who threatened him with a revolver. That other was a drunk and a degenerate. What about your promise? Are you still ready to go through with that phony marriage with me? I have no more reason to go to Palestine. But what shall I do with my bastard?"

And Stefa indicated her belly.

"We can still go to Palestine," I said without thinking.

"What will we do there? Yes, so be it. We'll find some kind of work. All I must do is wait till my parents die which I hope will be soon. My mother is sick from head to toe. Nor will my father drag around for long once she is gone. All they ever wanted was a little satisfaction from their children—some satisfaction they got! Why Jewish parents require so much satisfaction from their children is something I'll never understand. They don't have lives of their own. All their hopes are pinned on children and grandchildren. A crazy race. A sick race. Maybe it's not too late for an abortion. I'm in my fifth month. If I should get blood poisoning it wouldn't be any great loss either."

"No, Miss Stefa, don't do that to your parents!"

"Don't play the saint with me. You're not so holy yourself. All men without exception are the worst kind of egotists. They'd trample on corpses to gain their merest whim. Why would you want to do this? You can be frank with me."

"There is still the chance it might save me from the draft."

"No, not even the slightest chance. I told you you'd have to get papers, but so far you haven't done a thing. Without

documents you won't get a passport. I offered to pay your
expenses to go to your father's town so that you could obtain an excerpt from the permanent population register, but
you kept putting it off. Each time you made up a different
excuse. The *starosta* here in Warsaw is in no hurry to issue
passports to someone like you who is due for conscription.
Especially a discounted passport. Everything proceeds at a
snail's pace with these bureaucrats. Don't interrupt me.
Somehow, you're just like Mark. You're completely lacking
in will. A portion of your brain is paralyzed. You told me
about a woman who is twice your age. What is there between you two? Are you in love with her? Is it that you
can't bear to leave her? If that's the case, why are you wast-
ing my time? One charlatan is enough—I don't need two.
Give me an honest answer."

"If I'm conscripted, I'd have to leave her anyhow. She is
sick besides."

"What's wrong with her? Well, it's all the same. You
won't be conscripted and even if you are, you'll soon be
discharged. You can as much be a soldier as I can be a
rabbi. I'll give you a thousand zlotys to marry me, then
after my bastard is born you can divorce me."

"I won't take any money from you."

"What is it with you—a sort of philanthropy?"

"I want to do it for you."

"The situation is such that I can't be in Warsaw when
the child comes. I'll have to go away somewhere and I'll let

them know about the child a few months later so that they can nurse the illusion that everything is in order. God cursed the female gender. He is an even greater antifeminist than Otto Weininger and Strindberg. You don't look like an actor, but you must try to play the role that the fiction has become a reality for you. I'll tell you something: After you came here the first time, my father said: 'This young man appeals to me more than that rogue Mark. I wish you were marrying him for real.' I laughed at the time but fate has a way of playing funny tricks. Are you ready to go away with me for a few weeks? We have to arrange it so that the farce is carried through one hundred per cent."

"I hope I can get leave from the magazine."

"Eh? You must know that you'd be saving the lives of my parents. True, not for long, but it's a *mitzva* anyhow. As you see I know the word *mitzva*. I'm not a complete ignoramus. I'm in such a spot now that anything can happen. You're yet liable to become a widower a day or a week after the wedding. I want to ask you something, but answer me truthfully. Do you love anyone? Did you ever love anyone? What about that woman who could be your mother—do you love her?"

"Yes, but—"

"What *buts* are there? Where you love there are no *buts*."

"The but is that I can love someone else too."

"Get him—a Yeshiva boy and he talks like a regular Don Juan. How many lovers have you had so far?"

"Only the one, Gina."

"At least you're honest, or so it would seem. Mark was a liar, a dreadful liar, a pathological liar. All the while he was writing me those burning love letters—they sizzled between my fingers—he was selling himself to some snob from England, probably a spinster that no one else wanted. If people can be such liars then life isn't worth a fig. You told me you were interested in writing and all that. Why are people such liars? What's the reason for it?"

"The reason is that laws are formed that are lies from the very start. Your Mark might have loved you and six other women at the same time. He couldn't sign a contract to love you all your life. He obviously had others all the while. I only wonder why you can't understand this."

"I do understand it, I understand, all right. I can understand everything—every thief, every murderer, every degenerate. But I can only love one person. From the day I met him I loved only him, thought only of him, and all my dreams were of him only."

"It's not his fault that his nature is different from yours."

"No, it's not his fault. You don't know what love is, that's why it's easy for you to defend him. Why you would want to play out this farce is something I can't understand either, but when one is drowning, he'll clutch at any straw and to me you are that straw. Go to my father and tell him you want to marry me. We won't do it here in Warsaw. We'll go somewhere else. We have relatives here and people who consider themselves our friends and I can't play out this comedy in front of a whole crew. You say you have a brother here. Someone told me he's a very talented writer."

"Yes, that's true."

"You'll have to keep this a secret from him. From your parents too. We'll go to Danzig and hold the ceremony there. The next day you'll come back to Warsaw as if nothing had happened. I'll stay there, as the saying goes, to drain the bitter cup. Only one hope is left to me—that I die in labor and he, my son, dies with me. You still believe in God?"

"Yes, I still do."

"If He exists, then He is a comedian. This whole world is one big joke. Has any philosopher or theologian yet described God as a comedian?"

"It says in the Scriptures: 'He that sitteth in the heavens shall laugh.'"

"Everything is in the Bible and if it's not in the Bible, it's in Shakespeare. Go in to my father. I have to laugh too."

And Stefa erupted in a laugh, then her face grew quickly grim.

4.

I had asked for a leave of absence from the magazine and it had been granted at once. I promptly regretted having done so for the editor's tone seemed to imply that the magazine could get along without a proofreader. To begin with, I overlooked many errors. Secondly, the editor and the writers could read their own proofs. The readers in the provinces could no longer afford to pay for their subscriptions and the postcards dispatched to dun them cost more than what they owed. A dreadful poverty reigned over the villages. The young people all strove to go abroad but the consulates of all the nations seemed to have conspired to grant no more visas to Jews. It was easier for Polish peasants to obtain them. There was a need abroad for coal miners, farm workers, heavy laborers, not for study-house striplings who took to commerce or tried to enter the universities. Besides, many of the young Jews were infected with Marxism and communism and they instigated the local workers to strike. A number of leftist-oriented Jewish youth had smuggled themselves into Soviet Russia, but rumors spread that they had been imprisoned or sent to slave camps in Siberia. In any case, they were never heard from again. The Trotsky opposition had already emerged in Russia and the Party and the population were being purged of deviators, both left and right. A number of Trotskyites who had fled the Soviet Union to Poland told tales of horror. All the prisons were jammed with political prisoners, people were dragged from their beds in the nights. Hundreds of thousands of kulaks and plain peasants had been exiled en masse to Siberia. At the Writers Club, Isaac Deutscher, the

editor of a Yiddish Stalinist magazine, was suddenly transformed into a Trotskyite and published an attack against
Stalin. The Stalinists at the Club labeled him a fascist, an
enemy of the proletariat, a counterrevolutionary, and an
imperialist lackey.

I knew this Isaac Deutscher and often had heated debates with him. He had called me the very same names
with which he was now being assailed. He told me with
brutal frankness that on the day of the revolution there
could be no neutrals. Whoever didn't line up on the side of
the masses would be treated as an enemy of the people. He,
Isaac, was an expert on Marxist literature, a 100 per cent
materialist. Compared to me, he was wealthy and worldly.
He had a well-paying job on the Jewish-Polish paper *Nasz
Przeglad*. He came from Cracow and spoke an excellent
Polish. Nor did he tremble at the thought of the draft as I
did. When his time came, he went off and soon earned cor-
poral's stripes even though—as I suspected it—he dis-
seminated the Communist propaganda among the soldiers.

To return to Stefa. It happened like this. That day Stefa
asked me to go in to her father and, ask for his daughter's
hand, Isidore Janovsky had gone off somewhere, I believe
to his ex-partner who had been bankrupted along with him.
I was supposed to phone Stefa the next day but when I
rang, no one answered. I called again and again and it
turned out that there was no one at home, not even the
maid. This seemed to me puzzling. Mrs. Janovsky, a sick

woman, hardly ever left the house. Had some tragedy occurred? Had Stefa tried to commit suicide? I went there and knocked on the door but no one came. Another day went by and still no one answered the phone. I had taken leave from the magazine and had risked losing my job because of this phony marriage, but my bride had vanished along with my prospective in-laws.

I stayed awake nights trying to arrive at some solution of the puzzle but I knew that no brain can foresee the surprises life can invent. Almost a week went by and still no one came to the door or answered the phone. I sought out the janitor and asked him what had happened.

He said: "Seems they went away somewhere."

"All of them?"

"Seems so."

And he turned abruptly away from me to talk to the mailman who had brought a registered letter. The janitor appeared to me to be acting in a suspicious manner and I harked back to the volumes of Sherlock Holmes and Max Spitzkopf I had read as a boy. I took a walk down the street. I had sought suspense, and fate had provided it to me. Stefa had spoken about murdering her parents and then killing herself and in my imagination I pictured the family lying in a puddle of blood.

Stefa had marked down my address in her notebook and the suspicion of the crime was yet liable to fall on me. The police might somehow discover that I had been planning to marry her. I pictured myself in the courtroom as the prosecutor described my depraved character. I had lived with a woman twice my age, I had tried to get out of serving my country, I was about to marry fictitiously the murdered Stefa. My writings were brought into court and the prosecutor showed them to be rife with sadism, eroticism, demonology. One of the witnesses for the prosecution was Sabina. She admitted in court that I had made love to her. The prosecutor asked her:

"Is it true that your cousin who lived with you was a Soviet spy?"

"Yes, it's true."

And I was condemned to death.

The day was warm and Leszno Street was crowded with pedestrians, mostly women. At the Writers Club I had often heard women speak about spring fever. They all agreed that spring in Warsaw could make one crazy with longing. Today was just such a day. The air smelled of lilac blossoms, cool breezes from the Vistula, and the Praga woods. The scents of the fields and orchards lying around Warsaw blended with the odors of newly baked bread, rolls, and bagels, roasted coffee, and milk fresh from the udder. The sky loomed clear and perfectly cloudless above the rooftops and although it was still early in the day, it reflected the deep night-blue of those climates where the sun doesn't set during the summer months. The women, looking elegant in their new dresses and hats, carried bunches of flowers and parcels bound in colored ribbon. They stretched in swarms like during Rosh Hashanah when they gather at the stream to cast their sins upon the waters. I looked each one over and they looked back with frivolous glances and something like silent consent.

Suddenly, I saw Isidore Janovsky approaching in a long black coat and matching derby. He took mincing steps and leaned on his cane. He apparently didn't recognize me since he looked straight at me without a change of expression.

I stopped him and he seemed to come awake. I said: "Mr. Janovsky, how are you?"

He hesitated a long while, then said: "I know you. You're the young man with the certificate."

"Yes, right."

Isidore Janovsky wavered again. "Stefa no longer needs a certificate."

"May I ask why not?"

"Stefa is getting married this week."

I felt myself blush. I wanted to ask to whom, but all I said was:

"Well, congratulations."

"Thank you."

And Janovsky placed his cane a step forward.

I got out of his way and he went past me, the father of a bride and proud in-law-to-be. I stood there and stared after him. Then I headed for the Writers Club.

5

1

Fate played with me and I played along. I could see clearly that it was leading me to disaster but I told myself that I was ready for this. Everyone lost to it anyhow. The mystery regarding Stefa had been cleared up. She had married Leon Treitler, a wealthy man, a father of two married daughters, a landlord, a partner in a textile factory in Lodz. Leon Treitler owned a villa in Michalin, a resort on the Otwock line, and all the while I had been trying to reach Stefa, the whole family had been visiting there. Soon after the wedding the couple left on a trip around the world. They were scheduled to return only after the Days of Awe. How this change had suddenly occurred was something I could not fathom. Did Treitler know that she was carrying another man's child and had forgiven her? Or had she tried to deceive him?

None of this had anything to do with me now. The Palestine Bureau had withdrawn my certificate and it appeared that I was fated to either serve in the army or commit suicide. I lived in a state of suspension. I both played with fate and at the same time observed the game, or kibitzed, as they called it at the Writers Club.

Following my leave of absence I was given my proof-reader's job back but both the magazine and the publishing house that backed it hovered on the brink of bankruptcy. The authors had rebelled against me and issued an ultimatum that if I overlooked any more errors they wouldn't contribute any more articles. They accused me of spite and indifference. I promised fervently and even took a solemn oath to be more careful, but things deteriorated from week to week. I read without knowing what I was reading. If I made an effort and managed to grasp their meaning, the writings seemed to me trivial and false. The reviewers would praise a book but I couldn't figure out why. When they condemned one, the condemnation seemed without basis too, often rife with personal antagonism. The poetry was full of rhetoric and banality. Many poets only strove to please the Communist party leaders and their cultural activists, who no matter how much they were fawned upon could never be appeased. The stories struck me as boring and written in one vein. Although the number of industrial workers among Jews in Poland was comparatively small—most Polish Jews being merchants, brokers, heder teachers, and employed in various handicrafts—the authors kept writing about Jewish factory workers and even peasants, a species that hardly existed.

Correcting this trash became for me a physical torment. I suffered headaches from reading and sometimes the lines began to leapfrog over one another or turn green, gold, or fiery and I feared going blind. Everything with me proceeded awkwardly and I clearly saw that this state of affairs was no mere aggregation of accidents but part of a somber design.

Gina began to ail and hint that her months or weeks were numbered. I begged her to see a doctor but she found a new excuse not to each time. I watched with alarm as she grew thinner, weaker, unable to eat. Her sexual urges had dissipated and were replaced by a kind of maternal or sisterly affection toward me. She began to act modest around me and wouldn't let me see her naked. She'd lie in bed with me and not utter a word. Lying beside her, I lost my power of speech too. Although I had never mentioned a word to her about Stefa, I had the suspicion that she somehow knew about her and bore me a grudge. But how could she have learned about it? Unless her late grandmother had told her.

Spring had passed and the heat waves started. My brother Joshua had gone to Svider for the summer along with his wife and children, Yasha and Josele, or Joziek, as his mother called him. My brother had rented a villa from the Yiddish writer Alter Kacyzna. Other Yiddish writers and journalists were also vacationing in the area. From earliest childhood I had felt a powerful desire to be with my brother. Now that I had begun to write I was anxious to show him my work and consult with him. My brother was more than willing to help me but I was ashamed to face him both on account of my dealings with women and because of my writing.

I also knew that my brother couldn't agree with my world outlook. He was far from an optimist but he wasn't as pessimistic as I. He had a wife and children. Like many other liberals he hoped that despite all its insanities, mankind would move forward not backward. But I spoke like a nihilist and a suicide and more than once I evoked his anger.

He had invited me to spend the whole summer with him in Svider but I couldn't mix with the writers, nor did I want to cause him embarrassment with my pessimism. I knew that the writers' wives whispered about me and slandered me among themselves. Such were the contradictions within my character that I could neither be alone nor stand others or manage to keep perfect secrets about my conduct. I waged a kind of personal conspiracy. In a sense, I practiced my theory that one could not proceed in a straight, direct fashion through the world but had to constantly smuggle himself through, or muddle through.

Around that time I had written a story called "In the World of Chaos." Its hero was nothing less than a corpse who didn't know that he was dead. He wandered across Poland, attended fairs, called on rabbis, even allowed himself to be proposed for marriage. He could not understand himself nor did others understand him until he came to a rabbi, a cabalist who resolved his mystery for him—namely, that he was dead and must lie in his grave rather than make a fool of himself with the ambitions of the living. The story ended with the rabbi telling him: "Unbutton your gaberdine and you'll see that you're wearing shrouds."

I never had this story translated, but I wrote a number of variations on it, such as the story "Two Corpses Go Dancing."

"In the World of Chaos" might have provided me my first direction as to style and genre. Somehow I identified with this hero. Just like him, I lived yet was ashamed to live, ashamed to eat and ashamed to go to the outhouse. I longed for sex and I was ashamed of my passions. I always felt that the story in Genesis in which Adam and Eve eat of the fruit of the Tree of Knowledge then grow conscious of their nakedness expressed the essence of man. Man is the only creature who is ashamed to be what he is. The whole human culture is one mighty effort to cover and embellish itself; one huge and complex fig leaf.

As far as I knew, Gina had never gone away on vacation, but that summer she told me that she had rented a room with a kitchen in a villa lying between Otwock and Svider, and if I wanted, I could come to stay with her.

This put me in a quandary. It was one thing to be secluded with Gina in a third-story flat on Gesia Street where no one visited or looked in through the door or windows. It was something else altogether to be with her at a summer resort where you lived on the ground floor, where the door and windows stood open, and where you spent most of your time outdoors surrounded by neighbors.

The villa where Gina had rented the room lay close to Kacyzna's villa where my brother was staying. To go out to a resort I needed a special summer wardrobe. Gina informed me that her place was close to the Svider River where the vacationers bathed and sunbathed along the shore. But this was hardly an attraction for me. I hated the nudity and noise of a beach. I was shy to undress even in front of men. Besides, my skin is so white that if I stay out in the sun for even a short while I burn and blister. Nor can my eyes tolerate the sun's glare. I asked Gina if the doctor had told her to go away for the summer and she replied:

"Yes, no, it makes no difference."

2.

My musings brought me no closer to any conclusions regarding the world nor my own duties toward God and man, but I enjoyed—I might say—philosophical fantasies: variations on Spinoza, Kant, Berkeley, and the cabala, along with my own cosmic dreams. Since time and space were merely points of view; since quality, quantity, and even existence itself were categories of reason; and since the thing in itself remained completely concealed, there was room left for metaphysical fantasizing. My God was infinite, eternal, and possessed of endless attributes, properties of which we humans could only grasp a select few. I didn't agree with Spinoza that all that we know of God are His extension (matter) and His thinking. I was sooner inclined to see in Him other such qualities as wisdom, beauty, power, eternity, and maybe too a kind of mercy that we could never comprehend. The cabalists attributed sex to God, and I more than agreed with them in this concept. God Himself and all His worlds were divided into he and she, male and female, give and take, a lust that no matter how much it was satisfied it could never be sated completely and always wanted more, something new, different.

Since man is created in God's image, man could learn more about God by looking within himself, observing all his aspirations, yearnings, hopes, doubts. I envisioned God as resembling myself. He got much, much love from the Shechina, His feminine counterpart, the angels, the seraphim, the cherubim, the Aralim, the holy wheels and holy beasts, from the countless worlds and souls, but this wasn't enough for Him and He also demanded love from insignificant man, the weakest link in the divine chain whom He exhorted: "And thou shalt love the Lord thy God with all thine heart, and with all thy soul, and with all thy might."

He wants love (as I do) regardless of whether He has earned it. He frequently punishes His creatures but He demands that they forgive Him and acknowledge that all

His intentions are of the best. He Himself keeps many secrets yet at the same time He demands total candidness and a full baring of the soul.

Now that Gina was in Svider, Stefa traveling with a husband she didn't love, and I sleeping alone all the time, I would waken in the middle of the night and give my imagination free rein.

"Think what you wish," I ordered it, "you needn't be ashamed before me. You can soar to the highest heavens or sink to the lowest abyss for in essence they are one and the same."

It wasn't the Logos that was in the beginning, but the oneness, the unity. In God, everything is united—infinite thought and infinite passion, the ego and the non-ego, the greatest pleasure and the deepest despair, all matter and all spirit. The infinite had filled all space leaving room for nothing else. God was omnipotent, but He suffered from restlessness—He was a restless God. At first glance, this seems a contradiction. How can the omnipotence be restless? "Is anything too hard for the Lord?" How can an all-powerful suffer? The answer is that the contradictions are also a part of God. God is both harmony, and disharmony. God contradicts Himself, which is the reason for so many contradictions in the Torah, in man, and in all nature. If God did not contradict Himself, He would be a congealed God, a once-and-for-all perfect being as Spinoza described Him. But God is not finished. His highest divine attribute is His creativeness and that which is creative exists always in the beginning stage. God is eternally in Genesis. Each time He lifts His gaze He sees chaos and He wants to create order. But creation is coupling and God must come together with His female aspects to produce birth. Male and female are contradictions that constantly yearn to unite, but the more they unite the sharper grow their longings and caprices.

I slept some, awoke, dreamed, and came to again. Although my dreams were rife with fear, with demons, evil spirits, wild cruelties, and scenes of horror, I awoke from them with a lust that astounded me.

I stood by the open window to catch a night breeze. The sky over the Zamenhof Street rooftops was filled with stars. I literally felt the earth revolving on its axis, rotating around the sun, wandering in the direction of a constellation which would take it millions of years to reach and at the same time racing along with the Milky Way toward a target only eternity knew what it was and to where it extended. *I am earth, I am the sun, I am the galaxy, I am a letter or a dot in God's infinite book. Even if I am an error in God's work, I can't be completely erased.* I tried to conceive the trillions, quadrillions, quintillions of planets in space, their individuality and the creatures that swarmed upon them, each with its own evolution, history, and passions. No, there was no death within this cauldron of life. Each atom, each electron lived and had its function, its ambitions, its unfulfilled desires. The universe shouted voicelessly. It sang a serenade to another universe. Not only I but the table in my room, the chair, the bed, the ceiling, and the floor all took part in the drama. A heat emanated from the walls. A shudder zigzagged down my spine.

I tried to speak to Gina through telepathy. "Are you awake too? Do you also stand by a window looking out at the nocturnal mystery? What's wrong, my love, what ails you? Don't die, Ginele, for all death is a lie, a misunderstanding. Besides, I need you and I know that no one can take your place. Our coming together is a page in God's novel and no one can tear it out. No one can ever kiss, attract and satisfy me as you have. I long for you, because we have already met who knows how many times and our lives are intertwined in such a way that it can never be severed. Our love commenced when we were still amoebas. We were fish in the sea, birds in the air, moles in the ground. We kneaded clay into bricks in Egypt. We stood at Mount Sinai together. Later, I was Boaz and you Ruth, I was Amnon and you Tamar. When Jeroboam disjointed the tribes of Jacob, you were in Jerusalem and I was in Beersheba but I smuggled myself across the border to search for you. I worshiped the Golden Calf and in your despair you became a harlot in the temple of King Manasseh. You danced before Baal and Ashtoreth and you bared your nakedness for half a shekel. For your betrayal I beat you the whole night but at dawn when the morning star emerged, we fell upon each other with a thirst that no sin could ever slake.

"Because three thousand years ago you lay with the priest of Baal, Chammor son of Zev, tonight I will lie with the maid, Marila, daughter of Wojciech. She waits for me in the kitchen on a straw pallet. Her belly is hot, her breasts are rigid, her groin is primed for me and for every male who comes her way. I know full well that this act will complicate our accounts even more, bring new reincarnations and maybe prolong the Diaspora, but even though free choice was bestowed upon us, everything is predestined. The divine ledger is manifold. Marila is the eleventh generation of a coachman who seduced the wife of a peasant, and I the thirteenth generation of a milkmaid raped by a squire. It's all noted in our genes. God toys with us; He experiments with us in a test of reward and punishment, omniscience and free choice. A year hence, Marila will marry her fiancé, the soldier Stach, son of Jan, and for me there also awaits somewhere an ovary and a womb that will give birth to my son or daughter. God is the sum total not only of all deeds but also of all the possibilities. Good night, heaven. If you can, have mercy upon me."

3.

A letter from my father had arrived at Gina's but since I seldom went there (even though I had a key) I didn't get the letter until days later. The letter read as follows:

To my dear son, the scholar and man of substance, long may he live.

After I've wished you peace, I inform you that I must come to Warsaw to see a doctor since I am, may it not happen to you, not in the best of health. I'm suffering from stomach trouble as well as hemorrhoids and may the Almighty take pity and grant complete recovery to all the ailing of Israel. I've been away from Warsaw so long that I don't know if any of my old friends are still alive since all kinds of misfortunes and plagues occurred during the war, heaven protect us, and I haven't received any letters from them in a long time. "Thou knowest not what a day may bring forth." I heard that a Dr. Sigmund Frankel in Warsaw is a great healer and they are all, as it is known, emissaries of God. I therefore ask you to get me an appointment for a visit with this doctor, and to meet me at the train that will leave, God be willing, on the evening of the 11th day of Tammuz and arrive in Warsaw on the morning of the 12th at 10 A.M. at the Danzig Depot. I'll have to find a room at some inn in the Jewish quarter where the food is strictly kosher and which isn't far from a house of worship. Best would be the old neighborhood where we once lived—on Gnonya or Grzybowska Streets, an area with which I'm familiar. I've written to my beloved son, your dear brother Israel Joshua, but his wife, my daughter-in-law, Gittel, wrote back that he is abroad on business and won't be back for several weeks, and the local doctor feels I should see a Warsaw doctor immediately in case there is some growth, God forbid, that must be attended to. I certainly would like to visit with your brother, my son Joshua, and his family when he returns safely, and to greet them all heartily, and in behalf of your mother and myself I wish you all long life. Your father Pinchos Menahem, the son of the saintly Samuel, blessed be his memory.

I read the letter and shuddered. What day of the month of Tammuz was this? Father had failed to indicate on what day of the week he was arriving. I had gone to Gina's flat to pick up a German-Polish dictionary I had left there and which I now needed for a translation I was doing. I began to search for a calendar knowing full well that Gina wouldn't have a Jewish calendar in the house. She didn't have a calendar at all. Father's letter had rattled me so that I left without the dictionary I had come for. Afterward, I wasn't even sure that I had locked the door behind me.

Once outside, I started looking for a stand selling Yiddish newspapers which would show the Jewish date on the front page. But there were no Yiddish newspaper vendors on Gesia Street or maybe in my confusion I failed to see them. As usual, funeral processions wound along, one after another. At the corner of Gesia and Franciszkanska Streets, I finally got a Yiddish newspaper and to my horror I saw that today was the 12th day of Tammuz! But the clock already showed twenty past noon. Was Father still waiting at the depot or had he wandered off somewhere? And if so—where? A feeling of despair came over me. Although it wasn't far from where I was to the Danzig Depot I tried to flag a cab. But they were all taken. A streetcar came by and I did something I had vowed never to do—I sprang aboard as it was moving and caught a blow on my knee.

The conductor turned to me: "Do you want to kill yourself or what?"

And he added:

"Idiots!"

I began to pray to God that Father would still be waiting, recalling at the same time the saying in the Gemara that praying for something that was in the past constituted a false prayer. On the other hand, if time possessed no objective existence and the past was merely a human concept, maybe this wasn't a false prayer after all. I sprang down from the trolley even before it had stopped and was nearly thrown under the wheels. I began to race toward the depot and near the entrance I spotted Father standing next to a white-bearded rabbi and another man. I ran up all breathless and cried out:

"Papa!"

"There he is!" the rabbi said, pointing to me.

I wanted to hug Father, to kiss him and apologize, but somehow the opportunity never came. He held out his hand in greeting. He seemed perfectly composed. He half-said, half-asked:

"You obviously were delayed."

"I just got your letter ten minutes ago. It came to an address where I'm no longer living. I just happened to drop by there to pick up a book I left behind. A miracle! A miracle!" I exclaimed, ashamed of my own words.

The other man spoke up: "What did I tell you? It's a good thing you listened to us and waited. Upon my word. Well, how does the saying go—All's well that ends well."

"Praised be the Almighty!" Father said. "I didn't know what to do. All of a sudden I recognized the rabbi from Kupiecka Street. It was really a stroke from heaven. We hadn't seen each other for years but I'm good at recognizing people."

He turned to me. "You should remember the Kupiecka Street rabbi. He used to visit our house. It was during the time that Nahum Leib Weingut wanted to take all us neighborhood rabbis into the official rabbinate. This was yet under the Germans."

"How could he remember me?" the Kupiecka Street rabbi demanded. "He was just a child then. My beard has turned completely white since. But I remember him well with his red earlocks. How long is it, eh?"

"I remember you, I remember you!" I exclaimed, overcome with gratitude for the fact that Father hadn't wandered off and I didn't have to go searching for him. "I even recall what you said at that time: 'If heaven wants us to be paupers nothing Nahum Leib Weingut does will help.'"

The old rabbi's face beamed and his cherrylike eyes grew youthful.

"Is that what I said? Some memory he's got, the evil eye spare him! Yes, I recall now. Like father, like son. You know what, Rabbi? Since we've met, it's a sign that it was fated. In which case, why should you go look for an inn? You'll be my guest. Thank God I have a spacious apartment. So long as the children were still with us, it was somewhat crowded, but the daughters married and the sons left home. That's the kind of world that's evolved. Children no longer want to live with their parents. A father is likely to moralize a bit and who wants to hear the truth these days? The days fly by and there's no one to exchange a word with. Rabbi, where will you find lodgings in Warsaw? Listen to me and come to my house. We'll take a droshky and your son can ride along with us."

"No, no I couldn't!" Father argued. "I'm deeply grateful to you but how does the saying go: 'A stranger is a burden.' The rich people have servants to help them but your good wife—"

As the two old friends bickered, I studied my father. He had aged and seemed to me shorter. The reddish beard was now half-gray and shrunken, his forehead was sallow and wrinkled. His back was stooped and his gaberdine hung loosely on him. I saw in Father what I had seen in Gina a few weeks before—that he was much sicker than he knew. His blue eyes reflected the ponderings of those whose time has come. After lengthy haggling, Father agreed to stay at the Kupiecka Street rabbi's house but only if he would be allowed to pay his expenses. This was for me a blessing. I wouldn't have known where to locate the strictly kosher quarters Father required nor did I have the money to pay for them. I barely had enough to cover the fare for the droshky.

From the depot to Kupiecka Street was a short ride. We

crossed Muranow Street, turned into Dzika Street, and soon were on Kupiecka. During the war all the houses had been allowed to go to seed. Some of the walls had to be buttressed with wooden beams to keep them from collapsing. We went into an apartment that reminded me of our own on Krochmalna Street years ago. The kitchen exuded the same familiar smells—chicory, onion, moldy bread, gas. We entered a room resembling Father's old study— almost bare of furniture—containing only a table, two benches, bookshelves, and a lectern. The *rebbetzin* had gone shopping. Both men began to discuss learned matters. I said good-by to Father and went to arrange his appointment with the doctor. Father apparently sensed that I was broke for he gave me the money to buy the chit for the doctor and threw in a few extra zlotys besides. I didn't want to accept them, but Father said:

"Take, take. I'm your father."

And he nodded his head at a truth as old as the world itself.

4.

I had purchased a chit at the doctor's which would allow Father a visit, but not until a week hence. Father had brought along a manuscript and although he was short of money for a printer, he discussed the possibility of its publication with me. Even as a young man he had undertaken the responsibility of defending Rashi on every point on which he had been challenged by the tosaphists. He had been working on this manuscript virtually his whole life. I had heard him discuss it even while I was in heder. One Purim when Father had had a drop too much, he began saying to me:

"What happens to a person after he is gone? What becomes of his money, his houses, his stores, his honors? But the Torah and good deeds accompany him to the other world. It's the greatest merit to write a book and to glorify the Torah. It is said of an author of a holy book that his lips speak from the grave."

He added: "I'm convinced that when I come to the other world, Rashi will be there to welcome me."

Father would only speak of himself so highly when he'd had a drop to drink. It seems to me that this was the first time that I, his son, felt the urge to become a writer.

Now Father confided to me that since he was already in Warsaw, he would try to publish his "Righteousness of Rashi," as he had entitled his manuscript. Since Joshua had gotten his job with the *Forward,* he had been sending money home every month and Father might have managed to save up a couple hundred zlotys. Still, he now had to pay the doctors, and he hardly had enough to publish the book. He had apparently also forgotten that the number of Talmudic scholars and Yeshiva students was declining. The Orthodoxy of Warsaw had involved itself deeply in politics and now issued a newspaper and held conferences and congresses. True, these were politics of religion, but still they had acquired the jargon and style of wordly politics. The Orthodox no longer wanted to send their children to dingy heders and Yeshivas, but instead built schools and academies complete with all the modern conveniences. The Beth Jacob schools for girls had also evolved, which was a novelty in Jewish religious history. Like all other parties, the Orthodoxy needed funds—huge sums to meet budgets. Father didn't understand the new ways. Why couldn't the teachers go on teaching children at home as they did for generations? Why couldn't a youth who wished to learn simply go into a study house, take a Gemara down from the shelf, and study? And whoever heard of teaching the Torah to girls? Father feared that this was all the work of Satan.

I strolled with him along Franciszkanska Street and we gazed into the windows of the religious bookstores. They were nearly all deserted. The Torah had fallen out of fashion. Who needed so many commentaries, interpretations, exegeses, books of sermons and morals? Who needed justifications for questions posed to Rashi by the tosaphists? Besides, other authors had already answered them. Father was fully aware that his sons, Israel Joshua and I, had become involved wth worldly literature. My brother had published several books and my name too had appeared occasionally in a literary magazine or even a newspaper. But

Father wouldn't speak of this and it seems to me that he didn't even allow himself to think about it. Father held that all enlightened books regardless whether in Hebrew or in Yiddish, were deadly poison for the soul. The writers were a gang of clowns, lechers, scoundrels. What shame and mortification he felt for producing such offspring from his loins! Father put all the blame on Mother, the daughter of a *misnagid,* an anti-Hasid. It was she who had planted the seeds of doubt, of heresay, within us. Father had one consolation—that we hadn't grown up ignoramuses. We had studied the Torah, and whoever once tasted the flavor of Torah could never again forget that there is a God.

At times, Father made a mistake and stopped before the window of a secular bookstore. They featured such works as *Crime and Punishment, The Polish Boy, Anna Karenina, The Dangers of Onanism, The Jewish Colonization of Palestine, The Role of the Woman in Modern Society, The History of Socialism, Nana.* Some of the book jackets displayed pictures of half-naked females. Father shrugged his shoulders and I could read his thoughts. That gentiles should surrender to such trash was understandable. They had been and still remained idolators. But Jews? . . .

Father didn't recognize Warsaw. Here came a long column of boys identically dressed in green tunics and short pants displaying bare calves. They carried long poles and wore caps with the emblem of the Star of David. They were followed by girls in short dresses also revealing naked calves. They all sang. These weren't gentile children but Jewish boys and girls singing in Hebrew.

"Who are they? What do they want?" Father asked in amazement. I explained that these were youths seeking to emigrate to Palestine.

Father gripped his beard. "To Palestine? Why are they holding sticks? Do they mean to hit somebody?"

I told him that they had dedicated themselves to sports or perhaps the sticks were meant to simulate rifles.

"What? They want to fight wars? With whom? And how can Jews fight wars? We are like lambs surrounded by wolves."

"How long can we go on being lambs?"

"What do you mean—how long? Until the Messiah comes."

"Jews are tired of waiting."

"Those that grow tired aren't Jews. 'They that wait upon the Lord shall renew strength.'"

We passed a Kiosk featuring a poster which read in large Yiddish letters: *"His Wife's Husband,* an operetta from America." Father stopped.

"What is this?"

"Theater."

"Well, well, well. Everything the Mishnah predicted has come true. High time the redemption came, high time. That which we are seeing are the pangs preceding the deliverance.

We strolled for a long time in silence. We had emerged onto Nalewki Street and passed the prison on Dluga Street, the Arsenal, as it was called. Outside, convicts swept the gutter watched by an armed guard. The inmates had yellow complexions, yellow-gray uniforms, and even the prison walls were of the same dingy dun color. One convict leaned on his broom and studied Father and me with a half-bemused, half-amused expression, his eyes two laughing slits. I imagined that this was no living person but a corpse which instead of being buried had been thrown into jail, and it now laughed at this blunder committed by the living.

"Father, what does God want?"

Father stopped.

"He wants us to serve Him and love Him with all our hearts and souls."

"How does He deserve this love?" I asked.

Father thought it over a moment.

"Everything man loves was created by the Almighty. Even the heretics love God. If a fruit is good and you love it, then you love the Creator of this fruit since He invested it with all its flavor. And if someone is a lecher and lusts for females, it was the Creator who bestowed them with their beauty and allure. The sage recognizes the source of all the good things and he loves that source. When the fruit rots, you no longer love it, and when the woman grows old and sickly, the lecher runs from her. The fool will not give any thought to where everything stems from."

"What about the evil things? What is their source?"

"There are no evil things. Death which man fears most is a great joy and a blessing to the just."

"What about suffering?"

Father was silent a long time and I assumed that he hadn't heard me, but then he said: "That is the greatest secret of all. Even the saints weren't able to fathom it. So long as man suffers he cannot solve the riddle of suffering. Even Job didn't arrive at the answer. Moses himself didn't know it. The truth is that body and pain are synonyms. How could there be free choice without punishment for choosing evil and reward for choosing what is right? Behind all this suffering is God's infinite mercy."

Father paused and then asked: "Is there a house of worship in the neighborhood? Time to say the afternoon prayers."

6

I.

The summer had passed but Gina still didn't return to
Warsaw. The secret was out—Gina was both consumptive
and anemic. The doctors felt that she would be better off in
a sanitarium but Gina didn't want to nor could she afford to
enter a sanitarium. She had rented a room outside of Otwock, in the woods and away from all neighbors. When I
came to visit her there, she told me frankly that she
wanted to isolate herself from people and all their affairs.
She had come there to die. She had given up her apartment
on Gesia Street for which she had received a few thousand
zlotys for surrendering the lease. Gina had estimated that
she could exist on fifteen zlotys a week. She belonged to a
Sick Fund which provided her medicines free. I had
helped her move her books, occult magazines, and the few
other necessary possessions to Otwock.

My fear of the draft had been removed—I had been
rejected for military service. The doctors had found my
lungs not in the best of order and Pilsudski had ad-
monished the army to conscript no more weak young men.
Rumors circulated that the colonels who now ruled Poland

weren't too eager to have too many Jews in the army since many of them were leftists. The leaders of the Polish parties—the NDK, the PPS, and the Peasant party—complained that Poland had become a dictatorship. Pilsudski ordered the arrest of Witos, Lieberman, and a number of others of his opponents and he made them stand trial. For some strange reason, the editor of the Yiddish newspaper *Der Heint* sent me to cover this trial and to write my impressions of it from the standpoint of a literary observer. This had been arranged by my brother, who since obtaining his position with the *Forward* had proven himself an exceptionally able journalist. The reports that he published in the *Forward* under the pseudonym of G. Kuper (his wife's maiden name was Genia Kupferstok) became famous among Yiddish readers in both America and Poland, where they were frequently reprinted.

I myself nursed ambitions to be a journalist and this assignment was a stroke of luck for me. I was issued a press card by my newspaper and was seated in the courtroom among the journalists facing the accused, who only a brief time before had been ministers of the Polish Government. I felt more frightened here than the accused. The chamber was small and it seemed to me that these well-known political figures gazed at me with mockery. The journalists ignored me. The court proceedings dragged along. They consisted of lengthy, boring readings of charges that no one took seriously. Although I needed both the money and the prestige this assignment offered, I decided one day that it wasn't for me. My brother was a bit disappointed that I was tossing aside such a good opportunity, but he left the decision to me. Politics was not my game.

Nothing had come of Father's plans to publish his manuscript. Dr. Frankel had written one or two prescriptions for Father but from Mother's letters I gathered that they hadn't helped. Father wrote curt notes but Mother's letters were longer. With my younger brother, Moshe, Father was studying such volumes as *The Teacher of Knowledge* and *The Breastplate of Judgment*, and it looked as if—after Father's demise—Moshe would take over his post. It was therefore necessary that he be married, since pious Jews like the Belz Hasidim wouldn't accept a bachelor rabbi. But it wasn't easy to find a match for Moshe. He was too pious. He had isolated himself completely from the world. He hadn't an inkling about business or about any other worldly matters. He shouted during prayer, clapped his hands, sang the chants of Nachman the Bratzlav Rabbi, went into religious ecstacy. Describing Moshe to me, Father called him a saint. He said that compared to Moshe, he, Father, was a sinner. But the Galician girls who had nearly all attended Gymnasium and read newspapers and Polish novels weren't too keen about a youth who at nineteen wore a wild beard and earlocks dangling to the shoulders, a gaberdine to the ankles, an unbuttoned shirt, and old-fashioned slippers. Moshe was tall, even taller than my brother Joshua; blond; with a rare white skin, big blue eyes, and well-formed limbs. He looked like the image of Jesus Christian artists had created. The gentiles in Father's town considered Moshe a holy man and that's what he actually was. Had there existed such an institution as a Jewish monastery, Moshe would have surely become a monk. The danger was that Moshe might remain without a job.

In the letters my parents wrote me, they kept wishing me to get married, but I was no better suited to be a husband than was Moshe. Like Moshe, I neglected my appearance. So long as Gina was around she kept an eye on me, sewed on my buttons, darned my socks, even washed out my shirts and drawers. She referred to me good-naturedly as an idle dreamer, as a scatterbrain. She would complain: "What's the point of fantasizing? You, my little colt, won't change the world. Since God plays hide-and-seek, you'll never find Him."

Now that Gina had departed Warsaw, I went about messy and buttonless, with torn shoes, I went days without shaving. My hair had started to fall out. The stiff collars I wore were either too tight or too loose.

I was still seeking some means with which to penetrate the barrier of the categories of pure reason, to comprehend the thing in itself and to find a basis for ethics. I still rummaged through libraries and bookstores in the hope of encountering some proof as to the existence of a soul, of an as-

tral body, of some remnant that lingered after the heart stopped beating and the brain stopped functioning. I had read a lot of occult literature but more and more I kept hearing how mediums were being caught in swindles. Books came out detailing how professional spiritists duped their victims. I had already heard about Houdini stripping the masks from a number of famous mediums who had made ectoplasm out of cheesecloth, fabricated phony photographs of ghosts, used cheap tricks to fool such serious scholars and psychical researchers as Flammarion, Sir Oliver Lodge, Sir William Crookes, and many others who desperately clutched for every scrap of evidence of the immortality of the soul. I often had the feeling that sooner or later the truth would reveal itself to me if only I didn't cease groping and hoping. My literary work, my interest in the epoch of Sabbatai Zevi and Jacob Frank, had driven me to search for volumes that described various miracles and wonders of nature. My own nervousness gave me lessons in the power of hysteria and in the force of autosuggestion, or self-hypnosis. My inner enemy constantly pressed me and I had to keep formulating ever new strategies to overcome him or at least keep him temporarily at bay. I had begun glancing into the works of Freud, Jung, Adler. If I found less information there than did others, it was only because our own moralists and authors of Hasidic volumes had been keen students of man and had in simple terms revealed the deepest conflicts existent within the human soul. They knew all the symptoms of hysteria and the whole schism of the spirit. Man had to maintain watch over himself all the time since every second posed a danger. The pit of crime and insanity yawned beneath us constantly. The Evil Spirit never grew weary of assailing us with theories, conjectures, half-truths, fears, fantasies, and illusions of pleasures intended to eradicate the greatest gift God had given us—free will. In all the centuries that the gentiles had waged wars against each other the Ghetto Jew had waged a war with his inner enemy, with that power of Evil that roosts in every brain and constantly strives to lead it astray. The Emancipation had partially (or gradually) put an end to this Jewish war. The Enlightened Jew had himself become a bit of the Evil Spirit thanks to his experience of wrangling with him. He had become a master of specious theories, of perverse truths, of seductive utopias, of false remedies. Since the gentile world needed its idols, the modern Jew had emerged to provide new ones. He grew so absorbed in this business of idolatry that he came to believe it himself and even sacrificed himself to it.

2.

I had chosen but two idols that I would be willing to serve: the idol of literature and the idol of love, but many of my colleagues both in and out of the Writers Club invariably served the idol of World Betterment. They hammered away at me: How can one be a writer if one isn't ready to fight for a better world, equality, freedom, justice, a world without competition and of eternal peace? The capitalist countries fought wars on account of oil. They kept putting up new munitions factories. The strongest among them seized huge areas of the earth. Within the groups, some individuals seized all the power under the guise of democracy while they preached offering the other cheek. How could an honest and sensitive person witness all this and still keep silent?

Well, but terrible tidings emerged from the land of socialism.

Isaac Deutscher, who had become a Trotskyite, revealed many Stalinist outrages in his little magazine—the slave camps, the liquidation of the old Bolsheviks, the rigged trials and purges which had already taken the lives of millions of innocent people. Was this socialism? Was this the ideal postulated by Marx, Engels, Lenin? Deutscher had overwhelming proof that Leon Trotsky would have handled things differently. I attended a meeting at the Writers Club at which this Isaac Deutscher was the speaker. The Stalinists tried to outshout him. They called him the renegade, fascist, sellout, capitalist bootlicker, imperialist murderer, provocateur. But Deutscher had a powerful voice. He pounded his fist on the podium and his audience of Trotskyites encouraged him with thunderous applause. He hurled sulphur and ashes at Stalinists and right-wing Socialists, at Fascists, and at such alleged democracies as America, England, and France.

Within the Jewish circles, he castigated the Zionists in all their factions and variations. What madness to want to turn back the clock of history two thousand years! Well, and from where had the Zionists concluded that Palestine belonged to the Jews? They gleaned all their information from the Scriptures, a book filled with miracles and legends. Deutscher said that the fact that Zionism could attract millions of Jews merely demonstrated the degeneracy and hopelessness of the bourgeoisie.

Among those who came to the lecture were Sabina and her younger brother, Mottel. Although Sabina was leftist-oriented, she hadn't yet decided whether she was a Stalinist, a Trotskyite, or an anarchist. Mottel was a fervent Stalinist and he had come to heckle and maybe even throw a rotten potato or egg at the speaker. Mottel was short and broad-shouldered, with thick lips, a broad nose like a duck's (he actually was nicknamed Mottel Duck), and small, piercing eyes under bushy brows. Mottel was something of a buffoon. He spouted jokes, and absurdities that evoked laughter. He had a low forehead and a thatch of pitch-black, curly hair. Mottel Duck had already served time at the Pawiak prison for his Communist activities. His sister told me that he carried a gun. He allowed his sister and mother to support him. He ran around with rich girls who were drawn to communism and he took money from them, allegedly for party causes. He was a big eater and able to quaff numerous mugs of beer and sleep fourteen hours at a stretch.

Sabina frequently complained to me: "How it happened that such a child should come out of our pious family is something I'll never understand. Unless he is a bastard."

I had resolved repeatedly and warned myself not to have anything more to do with this Sabina, but I did the opposite. My earnings were so meager that I could no longer pay for my room at the eye doctor's on Zamenhof Street and Miss Sabina proposed that I move in with her family. A room had become vacant in their apartment and the rent was half of what I was now paying. Sabina's mother would serve me lunches cheaply. We had already kissed and I knew that once I moved into her house she would become my mistress.

This Sabina didn't speak of romantic love as had Gina or Stefa. Sabina had read the works of such modernists as Margerit, Decobra, Zapolska, and she had a high opinion of Emma Goldman. She often derided the institution of marriage as antiquated and held that the man of the future wouldn't make contracts for lifelong love but would conduct himself according to the dictates of nature. Sabina had read some of my stories and she believed in my literary powers if I could only find the right direction.

Sabina spoke to me frankly. A young man was after her, ready to marry her, but the little love she had felt for him before had completely cooled within her. He wrote poems in Polish. He came from some town in the Lublin region. He had dropped out of the Gymnasium and gone off to Palestine where he had struggled for two years, suffered from malaria, and come back a dedicated Communist. He had been arrested twice. She couldn't drop him all at once since he was madly in love with her and was, despite his Leninist convictions, capable of killing himself. But if I moved in with her, sooner or later he would remove himself. There was even a chance he might smuggle himself into Soviet Russia or be sent there by the Party.

When Mrs. Alpert heard that I was giving up the room, she fell into a kind of panic. She was ready to keep me on without paying rent, she claimed. Her eyes filled with tears. She told me that I was the best boarder she had ever had. She thought of me as a son. To her, a boarder wasn't someone who merely paid his rent—she had to feel a rapport toward someone with whom she shared a roof. My name had been mentioned in a Polish-Jewish newspaper she read and it was an honor for her to have such a person in her home. How could I treat her this way? Marila the maid also flushed, and turned sulky and tearful when she heard I was moving out.

She complained to me: "What bad did we ever do you that you're running away from us? I always kept your room spotless, not even a speck of dirt. When you wanted tea or whatever, I was ready to get up in the middle of the night to serve you. I took care of your phone calls and all your dates. You're obviously drawn to one of those fancy young ladies of yours, but none of them will be as faithful to you as I've been."

I listened to these reproofs in amazement. It had never occurred to me that I was such a catch. I wasn't tall or handsome, and I spoke a poor Polish. Whenever I glanced in the mirror I always grew half frightened of my own face. The little hair left on my head was fiery red. My face was pale and often as white as that of someone who has just gotten up out of a sickbed. My cheeks were sunken, my ears flaring, my back stooped. Women constantly corrected my Polish, pointed out that my tie was crooked, that my trousers seemed about to fall off at any moment, and that my shoelaces were untied. I suffered from colds and no matter how many handkerchiefs I had, they were always soiled. I felt so touched by Mrs. Alpert's and Marila's reaction that I blurted: "Well, all right. I'll stay with you, my dears!"

In a second I decided to hold on to both rooms! This was pure nonsense since I didn't earn enough to maintain even one room. But somehow I had the feeling that a God Who tolerated my insanities wouldn't forsake me.

3.

When Sabina heard what I had done, she said that I wasn't merely deranged but also suicidal. The most important thing for a young writer was to have a clear head, not to have to constantly fret about money. Well, and what would I do with two rooms? I didn't have any possessions outside of my few books and manuscripts. I had nothing to move out and nothing to move in. The whole thing sounded like a bad joke. Sabina was ready to give me back the few zlotys I had given her as a deposit, but I wouldn't hear of it. My only fear was that my brother shouldn't find out what I was doing. He would have scolded me like a father. He would tell his fellow writers and they would have something to laugh at. Well, but I had already had two residences when Gina was still living in Warsaw. It seemed that my type of conspiracy required two addresses.

I awaited a miracle and a miracle came. I walked into the Writers Club and the woman at the door told me that the editor of the afternoon paper, *Radio,* had telephoned me. He had left a number where I was supposed to call him right back. Had my brother again tried to get me a job? No, this time it wasn't my brother but someone else who had told the editor of *Radio* that I had displayed a talent for writing. He had also mentioned that I could translate from the German. The *Radio,* like the other Yiddish newspapers, printed suspense novels. The editor had just acquired an exciting novel from Germany, where it had enjoyed a huge success. The problem was, however, that the Yiddish reader wouldn't accept a novel with a locale as alien as Berlin with its strange-sounding streets. The novel didn't have to be merely translated but adapted in such a way that the action was shifted to Warsaw and the heroes and heroines became familiar Jewish men and women.

On the telephone the editor proposed this revision to me. He told me to come to his office and I didn't walk but ran. I've forgotten his name, but his image is fixed in my mind —short, stout, with a round face, ruddy cheeks, and amiable, half-sleepy eyes. He was a favorite of the newspaper's owner, perhaps a relative of the owner.

He smiled at me with the geniality of one who wants to grant a favor and rid himself of a burden at the same time. He took a thick German book out of a drawer. It appeared to be a thousand pages long.

He handed it to me and said: "Glance through it!"

I read the first page and asked: "Will my name have to be used?"

"No names."

"Oh, this is a stroke of luck for me!" I gushed, knowing the whole while that it is poor business to show how eager you are for a job. I came from a house which knew of no diplomacy.

The editor said: "We'll give you sixty zlotys a week."

In those days, sixty zlotys came to no more than eleven or twelve dollars, but in Poland this was a big sum. Whole families got by on such an amount.

I said: "Really, I don't know how to thank you."

"Go home and get to work. You'll supply us some ten

thousand words a week. Write simply, in short paragraphs and with lots of dialogue. Don't use any difficult words. If you need an advance, you can get one right now."

"As you understand . . ."

"I understand that you can use it. If the novel catches on, you'll get more work from us."

"I'll do everything in my power."

He wrote out a slip of paper for me and showed me where to take it to a cashier, who handed me two hundred zlotys. I had been struggling along as a proofreader and translator and suddenly I had become rich, even if burdened down with work. Although I felt doubts about God, His benevolence and providence, I offered up silent praise to Him. No, the world was no accident, no result of an explosion or something similar, as Feuerbach, Marx, and Bukharin contended. Because I didn't want to disappoint Mrs. Alpert and Marila, God had sent me this source of income. But why didn't he reward deeds nobler than mine? Why did He allow poor people to jump from trolleys and lose arms and legs, or Gina to die of consumption, or innocent children to burn to death by falling kerosene stoves?

Afterward, when I told a journalist at the Writers Club what had happened, he told me that I was a dunce. The editor was paying me half of what other writers of this kind of work were getting.

"Why didn't you bargain with him?" he asked me. He advised me to call the editor and demand more. He was willing to bet that he would raise me at least forty zlotys a week on the spot. But I was too proud to do something like that. I had been raised to believe that haggling and praising your own work and asking for a raise after a deal had been made was beneath human dignity.

4.

We sat around the table with Sabina, her mother, and her two brothers, and we ate dinner. Bryna Reizel, as Sabina's mother was called, told stories of her hometown.

I listened to every word. I had been disappointed in philosophy, I hardly believed in psychology, and not at all in sociology, but I had come to the conclusion that many truths or fragments of truth were buried in folklore, in dreams, and in fantasies. Where thought isn't linked with any discipline, it's able to catch a glimpse behind the curtain of the phenomenon. Bryna Reizel told of some Polish squire who following the failure of the 1863 uprising confined himself to a coffin where he ate, slept, read books, and lived for the next thirty years. When he died, they found inside his straw pallet a fortune in gold ducats and a will leaving his entire estate to an old lecher, a former lover of his, the squire's, wife. She, the wife, had died twenty years earlier. Bryna Reizel spouted stories about dybbuks, werewolves, demons who celebrated weddings and circumcisions in attics and cellars, corpses who worshiped in synagogues at midnight and summoned frightened passers-by to join them.

Bryna Reizel was past fifty and had suffered much grief, yet her face had remained youthful. The words slid out of her small mouth as if of their own volition and she used Yiddish iolioms I had not heard for a long time or only encountered in old storybooks. Sabina and her brother Mottel winked to each other and at times even laughed at their mother. They didn't believe in such nonsense, but I and Bryna Reizel's younger son, Haskele, listened. Haskele suffered from scrofula. He had a large head, "water on the brain." He had been taken from heder at an early age and hadn't been able to get a job with an artisan. He did a girl's tasks around the house—ran errands, heated the oven, swept, and at times even washed the dishes. His eyes were whitish and unevenly set. Sabina and Mottel reminded me at every opportunity that Haskele was a victim of capitalism.

Winter came early that year. Soon after Succoth a deep snow fell and the frosts commenced. My worries about a living had ceased so long as the novel would run, but Sabina's brother Mottel accused me of contributing to yellow journalism. He read each day's installment and pointed out again and again that this was opium for the masses to lull them from the struggle for a just order.

Sabina's fiancé (as he was known in the house), Meir Milner, only sought to engage me in debates. He was blond, blue-eyed, snub-nosed. He worked a half-day as an assistant bookkeeper in a button factory. I had blurted out that I didn't believe in historical materialism and he had promptly become my enemy. He kept on needling me. In what, he asked, *did* I believe? In the League of Nations that had immediately after its formation begun to expire? In Wilson's hypocritical manifesto? In the Balfour Declaration which wasn't worth the paper it was written on? In the false promises of Leon Blum, Macdonald, Pearl, Diamond, Gompers?

I reminded him about the number of comrades who had gone to the land of socialism only to disappear, but Meir Milner shouted: "False accusations from fascist dogs! Lies fabricated by the reactionary pigs! Delusions of Trotskyite provocateurs!"

"Let them burn like a wet rag, slowly," interposed Mottel the wag, "there is one cure for them—to be made a head shorter."

"One death isn't enough for them!" Meir Milner snarled along.

For the countless time I grew astounded over the bloodthirstiness that had been aroused among Jewish youth after two thousand years of Diaspora, after centuries of ghettos. If Lamarck and his disciples were correct in that acquired traits are inherited, every Jew should have emerged a hundred per cent pacifist. Modern Jews and Muslims should be born circumcised. I read books about biology and was particularly interested in the debate between the mechanists and the vitalists, the Lamarckists and the Darwinists.

Late at night I went to sleep. It was a tiny room with a window facing a blank wall. It was half-dark in there even on the brightest day. There was no electricity in the house, only gaslight. I had taken on so much work that I was constantly behind.

I lay awake thinking about Gina. I had visited her during the Days of Awe—a sick woman alone in the woods and far from neighbors, from a store, and without a telephone. She sat there and waited for death. This was no longer the Gina I knew but someone else; completely unfamiliar to me. She had almost stopped talking. I tried to carry on a conversation with her about the supernatural but she didn't answer. Had she given up her belief in the immortality of the soul? Had she lied earlier about her communications with the dead and now no longer sought to deceive me? Or had she gained access to secrets denied the healthy? I had the feeling that whatever I said to her would constitute a burden.

I asked her if she wanted to accompany me to the synagogue to hear the blowing of the ram's horn, and she replied:

"What for?"

And soon there was nothing left to say.

I wanted to come to her bed at night. I hoped to rouse a passion within her and to make her talkative one last time,

but Gina said that she must sleep alone. Weak as she was, she had made up a bed for me on a cot in the same room where she slept. She put out the lamp and grew immediately silent. I didn't hear her breathing. During the day she occasionally erupted in a wet cough but that night I didn't hear so much as a rustle from her. She had apparently swallowed a number of sleeping pills and had sunk into a kind of coma. I was afraid lest she die in the night.

Strangely enough, she had formed a friendship with a woman in Otwock who was also consumptive and with whom she was more open and talkative. Genia's brother was a doctor in Warsaw. She came each morning to visit and brought food she had bought for Gina. Genia liked to talk. In the two days that I spent with Gina, Genia and I became so friendly that we kissed when I left. She told me that doctors—her brother concurring—had given her a year to live. She lived next door to a friend, a young man who was in the last stages of consumption and could last another six months at best. She confided to me that Gina was hardly as sick physically as she assumed. Doctors who had examined her had agreed that she suffered from anemia, but it wasn't the kind of anemia that necessarily killed. She had been prescribed injections and a diet of liver which she ignored. Gina no longer wanted to live. I knew that it was my fault. My leaving to take a room at Dr. Alpert's had convinced her that all the hopes she had placed in me had been foolish.

My having moved in with Sabina seemed to me even more than foolish. I had light-mindly broken up a match between two young people. I generally wasn't inclined to marriage and even if I had been, it certainly wouldn't be to someone like Sabina. Although I didn't follow in the path of my pious parents, I had retained an ideal of a wife as my parents conceived it—a decent Jewish daughter, a virgin who after the wedding would serve if not one God at least one man. In brief, a wife like my mother. I should have admitted this to Sabina, but I saw that she was tired of flighty affairs and that she longed with all her womanly instincts for a husband, a home, and children. She might have calculated that in time I might tear myself away from Poland. Since my brother was a correspondent for an American newspaper, I had some connection with America. Somewhere inside, the Polish Jews sensed that they were doomed. I knew full well that playing around with women meant toying with lives, but I lacked the character and the strength to heed the voice of my conscience. I belonged to a generation which no longer believed in free will and which based everything on circumstances, ideologies, and complexes.

That night I had slept an hour or two. Suddenly, I awoke. Sabina was bending over me and her hair brushed my face. She too couldn't live like her righteous forebears. Although she was a leftist and I was considered a rightist, we were united by the same passion—to seize every possible pleasure at any price before we vanish forever.

One day as I sat in my room at Dr. Alpert's trying to stretch the novel in the *Radio* so that I could collect my sixty zlotys another few months, Marila the maid knocked to announce with a smile and a wink that I was wanted on the phone by a "beautiful young lady."

I went to the phone and heard a voice that seemed familiar, yet I couldn't place it. I searched my mind, and the woman at the other end of the wire made fun of my poor memory and tried to offer me hints to help jog it. After a while she revealed her identity: the former Stefa Janovsky and current Madam Treitler.

We were both silent for a long while, then I asked:

"What did you have, a boy or a girl?"

"I had nothing. Forget it."

"Your parents—"

"Mother died."

"Mark—"

"He is dead too. Not really, but as far as I'm concerned. I beg you not to mention his name. I've forgotten him completely. But as you see, *you* I haven't forgotten. Isn't that strange?"

"If it's true."

"Yes, it's true."